WARRIOR • 147

US COMBAT ENGINEER 1941–45

GORDON L ROTTMAN

ILLUSTRATED BY ADAM HOOK

Series editor Marcus Cowper

First published in Great Britain in 2010 by Osprey Publishing,
PO Box 883, Oxford, OX1 9PL, UK
PO Box 3985, New York, NY 10185-3985, USA
Email: info@ospreypublishing.com

Osprey Publishing is part of the Osprey Group.

Transferred to digital print on demand 2014

First published 2010

Printed and bound by PrintOnDemand-Worldwide.com,
Peterborough, UK

A CIP catalogue record for this book is available from the
British Library

ISBN: 978 1 84603 579 1
PDF ISBN: 978 1 84908 289 1
ePub ISBN: 978 1 78200 052 5

Editorial by Ilios Publishing Ltd, Oxford, UK
   (www.iliospublishing.com)
Page layout by Mark Holt
Index by Margaret Vaudrey
Cartography by Map Studio, Romsey, UK
Typeset in Myriad Pro and Sabon
Originated by PPS Grasmere Ltd.

The Woodland Trust

Osprey Publishing are supporting the Woodland Trust, the
UK's leading woodland conservation charity, by funding the
dedication of trees.

www.ospreypublishing.com

Artist's note

Readers may care to note that the original paintings from which
the color plates in this book were prepared are available for
private sale.

The Publishers retain all reproduction copyright whatsoever. All
enquiries should be addressed to:

Scorpio
158 Mill Road
Hailsham
East Sussex
BN27 2SH
UK

The Publishers regret that they can enter into no
correspondence upon this matter.

Editor's note

All images in this book are the property of the US Army.

Measurement conversions

Imperial measurements are used almost exclusively throughout
this book. The exception is weapon calibers, which are given in
their official designation, whether metric or imperial. The
following data will help in converting the imperial measurements
to metric.

1 mile = 1.6km
1lb = 0.45kg
1oz = 28g
1 yard = 0.9m
1ft = 0.3m
1in. = 2.54cm/25.4mm
1 gal = 4.5 liters
1pt = 0.47 liters
1 ton (US) = 0.9 tonnes
1hp = 0.745kW

Abbreviations

CCC	Civilian Conservation Corps
CE	Corps of Engineers
CO	commanding officer
detcord	detonating cord ("primacord")
KP	kitchen police
NCO	noncommissioned officer
OD	olive drab
ROTC	Reserve Officer Training Corps
S-mine	*Schrapnellmine* (shrapnel mine – antipersonnel mine)
T-mine	*Tellermine* (platter mine – antitank mine)
XO	executive officer (second-in-command)

CONTENTS

US COMBAT ENGINEER 1941–45

INTRODUCTION

The US Army Corps of Engineers (CE) is among the oldest branches of the Army, along with the infantry, cavalry, and artillery. Engineer units have served in every conflict and proved themselves invaluable to the success of every operation.

Regardless, the Army only possessed a few understrength engineer units on the eve of World War II. The engineers then grew drastically along with the rest of the Army. From a couple of dozen units the engineers reached a strength of over 700 battalions; scores of brigades, groups, and regiments; and hundreds of separate companies. Engineer units were divided into two broad categories. Special units included bridge, pontoon, boat maintenance, topographic, map supply, service, camouflage, water supply, forestry, petroleum supply, railway operating (transferred to Transportation Corps in November 1942), airfield construction, landing boat, shore party, aviation (responsible for refurbishing airfields), and other battalions. General engineer units included combat engineers and general service engineers, the latter being construction units. While there were large numbers of engineer general service, construction, aviation, and other battalions made up of African-American troops, only 11 non-divisional combat engineer battalions were African-American.

The engineers were both a combat and a service support branch. One of the most numerous types of unit was the combat engineer battalion (the proper term was always "engineer," never "engineering"). These included divisional battalions and separate battalions augmenting other units. Every US division, be it infantry, armored, airborne, mountain, or cavalry, had an organic combat engineer battalion. Of course, their strength, equipment, capabilities, and means of transportation varied between the different divisions. Their missions varied too, dictated not just by the type of division they were assigned to, but by terrain, climate, and how the enemy fought. The experiences of combat engineers operating in North Africa, Italy, Northwest Europe, and on Pacific islands would be very different.

The engineers were instrumental to the success of the combat arms and an integral part of the combined arms team. Combat engineers were just as essential to successful operations as infantry, tanks, tank destroyers, and artillery.

RECRUITMENT AND TRAINING

Pre-military training

When World War II broke out America was far from a militarized state and there were few pre-military training programs. Some civilian-run military academies and high schools provided Junior Reserve Officer Training Corps (JROTC) programs, but there were only 295 schools with a few thousand students in 1939. Unlike ROTC at universities, which led to an officer commission, JROTC programs simply provided basic military orientation. By 1942 the JROTC had expanded, but there were only 72,000 cadets. Resources and instructors (retired officers and NCOs) were simply not available. Attendance of JROTC had no official benefit when former cadets entered the Army. Regardless of what instruction they may have undertaken, they underwent the same training as the other recruits. They received no advance in pay or rank. However, when new units were filled with recruits there were few NCOs available, and cadre and junior leaders would be selected from the ranks. Those few with JROTC experience were naturally assigned as acting squad leaders and would later be promoted. The Army had no NCO schools; individuals demonstrating leadership ability, technical proficiency, and the ability to motivate men were selected.

The Boy Scouts were by no means a pre-military training organization, even though German propaganda claimed they were (German Boy Scouting and similar organizations were banned in 1934/35, leaving the Hitler Youth as the only option). The Boy Scouts were extremely popular and while there was no military training, the boys learned scores of outdoor living and fieldcraft skills as well as responsibility, duty, and honor, all set against a patriotic background. Boy Scouting was definitely a benefit for future soldiers.

A program that would become very beneficial to the Army was the Civilian Conservation Corps (CCC). The CCC was established as one of the most effective economy-boosting New Deal programs by President Roosevelt and began operating in the summer of 1933. It became the single greatest conservation program in American history. Initially it was limited to men of 18–25 years of age who were from families receiving welfare, and allowed them to work on a wide range of public works projects and conservation programs. In 1937 the age limits were changed to 17–28 and their families no longer had to be on welfare.

BELOW LEFT
Engineers undergoing basic training within their unit. Pick-and-shovel work digging field fortifications and building roads in training areas did as much for physical fitness as practical training.

BELOW
Prior to World War II, Civilian Conservation Corps enrollees fell trees to build a national park recreational lodge using a two-man chainsaw, similar to the model used by the engineers. Many future combat engineers received valuable experience in the CCC.

The operation of the CCC was placed under the Army, but the program's different aspects were administered by the Departments of War, Labor, Agriculture, and the Interior. The future World War II Chief of Staff of the Army, Colonel George Marshall, organized the CCC using military principles. It was *not* a militarized organization however. The CCC was organized into thousands of companies in camps in every state and territory in national and state parks and forests, and in public lands. "Enrollees" wore unadorned World War I olive drab (OD) and khaki uniforms, blue denim work uniforms, and later, spruce green civilian-type work clothes.

They were organized into squads and platoons, had roll-call formations, lived in barracks, and ate in mess halls. That was the extent of the CCC's militarization; there was no military training. Regular Army and Army Reserve lieutenants and captains commanded the 100–200-man companies, but the platoon and squad leaders were selected enrollees demonstrating leadership skills, and they doubled as foremen. Administrators, education advisers, and conservationists were also assigned. Cooks were initially provided by the Army, but they trained their replacements from among the enrollees. They were fed the same garrison rations as the Army. Early on, 70 percent of the CCC was malnourished and undereducated. Outdoors living

Engineers operate a rock quarry. Here can be seen two crawler-type power shovels and a gravel crusher. The power shovels are loading rock into dump trucks for a short trip to the dump ramp behind the crusher. The resulting gravel is hauled by other dump trucks to worksites, to be used to repair roads or perhaps surface an airstrip.

and work, camaraderie, and good food changed that. High school equivalency classes were held in the evenings presented by graduated enrollees and local volunteers. When ready they took state high school examinations.

The work that "Roosevelt's Tree Army" performed greatly helped the country's infrastructure and economy. They reforested clear-cut lands, planted billions of trees, restocked lakes with fish, improved erosion control, undertook disease and insect control, fought brush and forest fires, fought floods, strung telephone lines into remote areas, and undertook many other projects. They also built roads, bridges, fire observation towers, culverts, flood-control dams, drainage systems, and park and recreational facilities. Thousands of enrollees trained as carpenters, truck drivers, radio operators, mechanics, surveyors, typists, electricians, plumbers, and welders. The fact that millions of young men were usefully employed by the CCC during a period of extreme hardship is credited with a drastic reduction in crime.

Much engineer work was a matter of picks, shovels, and strong backs. The old reliable D-handle shovel was a tool that all engineers became familiar with.

By the end of 1935 there were over 500,000 enrollees in 2,600 camps. They enrolled for six months and often extended this for one or two additional periods. The pay was $30 a month. They kept $5 and the rest was sent to their families. The average camp purchased $5,000 of food and goods a month in cash-strapped local communities. There were no mutinies, revolts, or strikes and bad behavior and "desertion" led to "dishonorable discharge," which could affect future job prospects and let down their families, who counted on the money they earned. Young men learned to sacrifice for the good of others and to live and work together. "We're going to leave morally and physically fit to lick Old Man Depression" was a motto. Most former enrollees have nothing but good memories of their CCC experience.

By 1941 with many projects being closed down the CCC was reduced to 200,000 men living in 900 camps. With the national emergency declared after war in Europe broke out, increased job opportunities as the nation's economy improved, increased war material production, and expansion of the armed forces, there were fewer applicants. Enrollees were leaving to take advantage of increasing job opportunities. Much of the CCC was redirected to build military posts. With war declared in December 1941 it was decided to disband the CCC in July 1942.

The benefits derived by the Army from the CCC were immeasurable. Over 3 million youths had enrolled in the CCC during its nine-year existence. A majority would serve in the armed forces or war-related industries and services. It had made them fit and had educated many, teaching them self-sacrifice, self-discipline, and self-confidence; they had learned to live in group situations, and gained many skills valuable to the armed forces. The skills learned in the CCC were particularly valuable to the engineers, and engineer units had a high percentage of former CCC enrollees. Their experience gave many an edge in promotions and it can be said that the engineers' NCO corps had a core of former CCC enrollees.

Conscription

The Selective Training and Service Act signed into law on September 16, 1940 authorized peacetime conscription. This was in response to the "limited emergency" declared when war broke out in Europe a year earlier. The act provided for 12 months' service. All males aged between 18–65 were to register and those up to 45 were liable for induction, although the maximum age of induction was 38. In late 1941 after the President declared a "full emergency" the draft period was extended to 18 months. The draft was conducted by a national lottery. After draft registration numbers were assigned a drawing was held on October 29, 1940. A total of 365 capsules were drawn at random and the numbers announced in newspapers. Each day of the year was assigned a number from 1–365. Physically qualified individuals were called up in the order their birth date was drawn. This was repeated each year with the age bracket moved up until the draft was cancelled in 1947. When their number was drawn the men received an eight-page questionnaire used to determine their eligibility for military service. Most inductees and volunteers were born between 1919 and 1926.

There were deferments and exemptions based on physical qualifications, religious grounds, and essential employment, which included defense industries and farm workers. This was determined by local draft boards. There were no education exemptions although college students undertaking ROTC or other officer training programs were deferred. Nor were there exemptions for family hardships such as caring for ill or elderly parents.

This treadway bridge, with storm boats serving as pontoons, allows a 2½-ton dump truck to cross. Note the treadway sections extending beyond the bridge to cross marshy ground. These sections would be supported by cross logs.

In December 1942 voluntary enlistment in all armed services was ordered to cease. This provided a more efficient means of mass induction. There was a final rush to volunteer before the order took effect on January 1, 1943. Most volunteers had enlisted during the first few months after the Japanese attack on Pearl Harbor.

Young men could be ordered to report for their induction physical as little as ten days before the reporting date. They would report to their draft board and then be taken by bus or train to the nearest Armed Forces Induction Center, usually at a major city post office or federal building, for a physical and paperwork. Those who were selected were assembled and if they desired were sent home for a week to put their affairs in order. Most accepted this option, but could be sent straight on to the reception center if they desired. The others would return the next week and take part in a mass swearing in.

During pre-war maneuvers an M3 light tank and Dodge ½-ton command car ford a bypass beside a now-ready H-10 portable bridge, which was not used during the war.

They might travel by bus or train to a military base anywhere in the country, where they then reported to a reception center. There they were processed, given a physical, tested (with the Army General Qualification Test, or AGQT), inoculated, issued uniforms, and classified.

This last step was important. Recruits were interviewed by a classification officer or specialist who determined their job assignment. Besides the results of the AGQT the classification system took into account age, physical hardihood, mental endowment, education, occupational skills, ability to assume responsibility, and aptitude. Creating an army of millions and with little time meant that an individual's civilian job skills would be utilized to the maximum extent. Specification serial numbers (SSNs) were assigned to every military occupation specialty. An SSN below 500 had a corresponding civilian job, and this included most engineer Military Occupation Specialties (MOSs). Such civilian jobs included carpenter, framer, painter, cabinet and furniture maker, electrician, plumber, draftsman, construction equipment operator, logger, demolitioneer, ditch digger, rigger, utility repairman, surveyor, boilermaker, machinist, mason, bricklayer, concrete worker, riveter, sheet metalworker, and steelworker among others. The engineers also needed truck drivers, mechanics, and welders. After three days to two weeks at the reception center they would be assigned to a unit or training center somewhere to begin their training.

Dog tags

Each soldier was issued two identity tags ("dog tags") worn around the neck on a beaded chain or cord. Prior to the Pearl Harbor attack, ID tags served only as a means of identifying remains. The rectangular stainless steel tags, with rounded ends, bore the individual's last and first names, middle initial, eight-digit serial number, and the next-of-kin's name, street address, city, and state. From November 1941, the year the soldier received his tetanus inoculation (T42 for example), his blood type (A, B, O, or AB), and religion (C for Catholic, H for Hebrew, and P for Protestant) were added. Many Jewish soldiers opted not to enter "H." These additions made the ID tag a life-saving aid. In July 1942 the requirement for the next of kin's name and address was rescinded for security reasons. There were soldiers whose next of kin resided in Germany or Italy and it was feared they would be harassed. Serial numbers were assigned according to category: the 10,000,000-series to enlisted volunteers, 20,000,000-series to National Guardsmen, and 30,000,000-series to conscripts. Officer serial numbers were preceded by an "O." If killed, one dog tag was to remain with the body and the other turned in. From 1939 onwards the end of the tag had a notch. Myth says this was for inserting the tag between the teeth of deceased soldiers. This was not its purpose. The notch fit over an aligning pin in the Model 70 Addressograph machine used to print the tags.

Basic training

Engineer battalions, as with most other units in the era's rapidly expanding Army, were basically created from scratch. Engineer battalions were being raised at a rapid rate at posts scattered across the country. The existing engineer combat regiments were broken up in the spring of 1943 to accommodate the Army's new unit pooling concept. Rather than regiments with a fixed number of battalions they were broken up into separate battalions for attachment to groups that could control any number and type of battalions and companies as required by the mission (the infantry was one of the few branches to retain regiments). The regiments' two battalions became separate combat engineer battalions receiving new numbers and the regimental headquarters often became an engineer combat group headquarters, which retained control of the two original battalions. Once deployed, another battalion and other engineer units would join them. Other, separate battalions were raised from scratch. Divisional engineer battalions were raised with their parent divisions.

Newly activated units were organized by assembling a cadre of officers, NCOs, and specialists. A few experienced officers were reassigned from other units to provide their leadership expertise. This included the battalion commander, possibly one major, and perhaps only two captains. The rest of the officers were almost all newly commissioned 2nd lieutenants from ROTC and the Engineer Officer Candidate School (OCS) at Fort Belvoir, Virginia. They were known as "ninety-day wonders," and the OCS graduates often had only high school diplomas. Very few of these newly minted "butter bars" had any military or civil engineer education. Those who did were considered highly valuable. Even those attending Engineer OCS had learned no military engineering; OCS had only taught them to be officers with an engineer twist. Ideally there would be enough engineering-educated officers to assign one to each line company and a couple to the battalion staff. Seldom were there even that modest number and the commander made the decision whether to place them on the staff or to "load" the companies. The companies certainly needed the benefit of their expertise with coming training, but the staff too needed engineering and planning expertise. Among all these inexperienced, newly minted lieutenants the real stars amongst them would be selected as company commanders and staff officers and promoted over their peers.

The cadre's NCOs were the real gold when organizing a battalion. Many of these men were career Regular Army NCOs with four or more years of experience in engineer units. They knew more about military field engineering than officers with engineering degrees, knew all the tricks of the trade, and

BASIC ENGINEER TRAINING

All squad members were cross-trained in one another's skills. Here, after learning to operate the Mall Tool Company Model 6 chainsaw to fell trees, move fallen trees, construct an A-frame and then a double A-frame gantry from available materials, and using the hand tools from a pioneer tool set, they learn the skills of a rigger. They are using double blocks and tackle to hoist heavy weights. They'll then use the logs to construct a bridge. The buck sergeant is one of the cadre instructors. The soldier with the navy blue brassard bearing corporal chevrons is a recruit himself appointed as an acting corporal ("acting jack") and may well end up becoming a squad leader and sergeant. During basic training acting corporals were appointed to lead squads and acting sergeants served as platoon sergeants. They wear the woolen service uniform with steel helmets (which doubled as hard hats for construction work), service shoes and leggings, and heavy leather work gloves not issued to other troops.

Field marching order with overcoats. While equipped with the new M1 rifle, this unit still has the "dishpan" M1917A1 steel helmet, which was commonly worn in training through 1942.

how to work out problems. They knew how to manage men and units. They knew when to place the men and their officers under pressure and when to let up and reward them. They knew how to keep a unit on an even keel, so long as there were no officers trying to control every little detail. It was not uncommon for a given cadre of NCOs to have started up several battalions in succession, whilst remaining together as a group. Once they worked a unit up and ran it through its basic and unit training they would go on to another unit. Eventually the deployment cycle would catch up with them and they would deploy with the unit. They were vital in order to start up units, and they would have a great deal of influence and effect on the training and development of the unit's NCOs.

The unit's cadre was also composed of specialists. This was a small group of equipment operators, radio operators, clerks, automotive mechanics, drivers, cooks, supply specialists, and so on. Most of these men had been in the Army for several months and had completed basic and specialty training at training centers. They too would help train specialists and would themselves stay with the unit. After completing their basic training, some recruits within the unit would be sent off to schools for specialty training. Some would return to the unit. Others would be reassigned elsewhere according to "the needs of the service." Other trained individuals would be assigned to fill their slots.

Newly raised battalions conducted their own basic training presented by the cadre. It might take weeks for a unit to assemble its personnel as they arrived from reception centers. The main draft of recruits was usually from a particular state or region, but smaller groups would arrive from other states.

As the unit was filled with recruits the cadre NCOs kept them busy with drill, physical fitness, and lectures, and there were plenty of work details to get the newly built unit area in shape, plus kitchen police (KP) and guard duty. They also learned the nuances of barracks life: stowing their uniforms and gear in the prescribed manner in lockers, displaying them for inspections, making their bunks properly, barracks cleaning, and so on. There was a great deal of in-processing and administrative work. The most important part of this was the work of the classification clerks. They studied each man's records and assigned him to a slot that could make use of his past work experience. The engineers received a great many men who had some type of construction experience, from ditch digging to carpentry to electrical work. Skills and personal desires could not always be matched to duty positions.

A lot of preparation had to be undertaken before training began. Training schedules were developed, training areas and ranges requested, training aids and equipment collected, instructors and support details

A posed photograph of part of a platoon advancing during a field training exercise. In practice they would be much more dispersed.

Engineers prepare demolition charges to destroy enemy ordnance. In the wooden crate the rectangular box contains 10 non-electric blasting caps and the tubular one has four M1 friction igniters.

assigned, and so on. As the unit assembled and even weeks and months after the unit was raised, long-requested equipment and supplies trickled in. With literally thousands of units being raised all over the country there were often shortages and delivery delays. It was not uncommon for units to begin training with serious equipment shortfalls.

The 13-week Army Mobilization Training Program for basic training was similar for all branches. It might take up to three weeks longer because of insufficient training areas and ranges owing to the large number of units competing for their use, equipment shortages, weather delays, and the need for remediable training.

Basic training taught recruits a full range of subjects to allow them to function as soldiers. While the NCOs were hard on the troops, making unrelenting demands for perfection, it was not always the depersonalizing experience imagined by many. In many cases the NCOs would remain with the unit and developed more amenable relations with the troops. There were numerous changes in the training program during the course of war based on lessons leaned in combat, the introduction of new weapons and equipment, and standardization between branches. In 1943 basic subjects included:

Military courtesy and discipline
Articles of War (military law)
Military field sanitation
First aid
Personal and sex hygiene
Defense against chemical attack
Practice marches and bivouacs
Dismounted drill (with and without arms)
Equipment, clothing, and tent pitching
Interior guard duty
Hasty field fortifications and camouflage
Elementary map and aerial photo reading
Physical training
Inspections
Protection of military information
Organization of the Army

OPPOSITE
An M2 truck-mounted 40,000lb-capacity Loraine crane is used to construct a replacement timber bridge.

A great deal of time was spent on the rifle, including assembly and disassembly, care and cleaning, basic marksmanship, firing positions, sighting, range estimation, and range firing. This included zeroing the rifle (adjusting the sights to align with the bullet's trajectory), firing on known distance ranges, and for qualification. Soldiers would be awarded the Marksman, Sharpshooter, and Expert Badge depending on their qualification score. They learned about the carbine, hand and rifle grenades, landmines, and booby traps.

Physical fitness training was conducted daily in many ways. They became intimately familiar with the Army "daily dozen":

1. Side straddle hops ("jumping jacks")
2. Pushups
3. Cherry pickers
4. Rowing exercise
5. Side benders
6. Flutter kicks
7. Toe touches
8. Crunches
9. Trunk twisters
10. In-place double-time
11. Standing leg lifts
12. Lying leg lifts ("six inchers")

Training schedules frequently included runs of 1–5 miles in formation, forced marches of 5–20 miles with equipment, and obstacle courses. In the field they dug foxholes and had to refill them before displacing. Bayonet training was given more for instilling aggressiveness, coordination, agility, and physical conditioning than the possibility that they might use cold steel in combat.

Basic training included training soldiers in their specialties. Much of this training was done collectively. For example, an engineer squad contained six different specialties in addition to the leader and assistant leader. The bridge carpenters, general carpenters, electricians, drivers, demolition men, jackhammer operators, utility repairmen, and general riggers (specialized in lifting and moving large or heavy objects with block and tackle) within a company would be collected together and provided training. Often, after being given a manual to study, a civilian-experienced jackhammer operator or electrician would find himself training his fellow specialists. Once they had learned the basics of their jobs they learned more about working and training as part of their platoon.

As training progressed they undertook basic squad and platoon movement formations, defensive and offensive tactics, tactical live-fire exercises, and practiced defense against air attack. Engineer specific training included the use of engineer tools, rigging, placing and removing landmines, demolitions, road repair and maintenance, obstacle construction, booby traps, route and bridge reconnaissance, and fixed and floating bridge construction and repair. Regardless of the specialties assigned to individuals within squads they were cross-trained to some degree in all skills. Demolitions training was especially popular, although there was a considerable amount of danger involved. They blew up bridges they had built in training, blew down trees, blew stumps out of the ground, cratered roads (and repaired them), cut railroad rails and pipe, and so on.

In an unusual arrangement, a Bailey bridge is floated on pontoon boats. Some of the boats have 40hp Evinrude outboard engines mounted. These would have to be run constantly to hold the bridge in place, which was not an ideal situation. An M2 medium tank is crossing.

As the battalion completed basic training the recruits found the NCOs were not so hard on them. There was a big beer party, and individuals began to be promoted into NCO slots. They were now ready to start basic unit training as a combat engineer battalion.

Unit training

Unit training saw companies operating with their platoons. Much of this instruction had to do with bridge building. They would team up with different types of bridge companies and learn how to erect bridges day and night regardless of the weather conditions. There is more to erecting bridges than meets the eye. The site must be reconnoitered and be accessible to vehicles. That means the banks cannot be too steep, and the ground must be firm enough to support vehicles and be free of trees, dense brush, or rocks. If these conditions were not found, considerable preparatory work was undertaken. The same applied to the far side. Vehicles had to be able to exit the site and a route had to be available to use as a road. If work was needed on the bridge's exit site then equipment and troops might be ferried across to begin work and have it completed by the time the bridge was erected.

The Army employed three principal types of tactical bridges. The smallest was the M1938 infantry support footbridge operated by engineer light pontoon companies. This was a narrow footbridge with 12ft sections up to 400ft in length, erected on small pontoon boats. The M1 treadway bridge was a heavier pontoon bridge with a 40-ton vehicle capacity including tanks. Treadways consisted of two separate roadway sections supported by pneumatic pontoons. It could be of just about any length; 1,000ft treadways were used to span the Rhine. The British-designed M2 Bailey bridge was delivered by Bailey bridge companies. It too had a 40-ton capacity, but it could be constructed with one or two addition panels stacked atop one another to greatly increase its capacity. It was assembled using sections 10ft long and 12ft wide. Its length was limited to 180ft without supports. Behind the lines engineers constructed standard timber bridges, which usually replaced tactical bridges so they could be sent forward for future operations.

They also built corduroy roads, which proved critical in Europe. These consisted of logs 6–8in. in diameter and 13ft long, laid perpendicular across the roadway to support traffic on muddy ground. On softer ground

Engineer training could be quite technical. Here a topographical survey party sets up a theodolite and prepares its plotting board in order to undertake a survey to determine a precise location.

five log stringers were laid beneath the road surface logs parallel with the traveled way. On particularly soft ground log sleepers were laid beneath the stringers at 4ft intervals perpendicular to the roadway. The log road surface was edged with curb logs and staked in place, and was often covered with a layer of earth or gravel to soften the bumpy ride caused by the washboard effect.

The next phase of training was combined training. The engineer battalion began training alongside other divisional units and performing tasks in support of them as they undertook their own training. Battalion elements would conduct route and bridge reconnaissance, erect bridges, lay and clear inert mines, and construct roads and supply trails. Squad, platoon, and company tactical training was accomplished, which included urban combat exercises.

Live-fire exercises were included, as well as an infiltration course. This was a 50 x 50yd area of barbed wire, mud holes, and craters with small demolition charges that were periodically detonated. At one end was a deep trench. A platoon at a time was taken into the trench and each squad went over the top in sequence. They low-crawled to the far end where two or three machine guns were positioned. They fired streams of tracers over the crawling troops some 3ft above the ground. Flares would occasionally pop over the area causing the crawling troops to freeze until they went out. It provided a realistic feel of what battlefield conditions felt like and served to instill confidence.

Much of this training was in conjunction with regimental and divisional maneuvers as well as large-scale army maneuvers. This necessitated moving the unit and all its equipment to distant maneuver areas, usually by rail, which was itself part of the training. Competitive training exercises were held between companies and platoons, and included bridge building, obstacle breaching, minefield laying, and tactical firing.

Training was never fully completed. It went on until the unit deployed overseas and unless immediately committed to combat, training would continue. Prior to deployment the over-aged, physically unfit, and those with recurring medical problems were reassigned. Equipment shortages were made good and newly authorized replacement equipment was issued.

DAILY LIFE

Barracks life

Reveille was at 0500hrs, with a short time allowed to wash and shave, dress, and don the prescribed gear. There would be a company roll-call formation, then breakfast, and this was followed by some form of physical fitness training for two hours, a "short" march or run, the Army "daily dozen," or simply dismounted drill. Whatever training was scheduled for the day was undertaken until noon, when lunch was served. Training would continue until after retreat was sounded at 1700hrs. Dinner was served and the troops might be off for the evening, but there was often more training until 2000hrs or 2200hrs or barracks cleaning. It was not uncommon for a unit to undertake, for example, footbridge construction during the day and then repeat it at night. Taps was sounded at 2200hrs and "lights out" soon followed. Saturdays were also a training day, but they often involved inspections, equipment and barracks cleanup, and administrative necessities. Sundays

---

Garrison diversions

Card games were quite popular, the most common being varieties of poker. "Acey-ducey" and other backgammon games were popular as was bridge, the latter especially among officers. Solitaire, played by oneself, was a common pastime when serving as charge of quarters. Checkers and dominos were widely popular and chess less so. Craps and other dice games were common, especially aboard troop trains and ships. Gambling stakes in both craps and poker were not very high owing to the low salary. Units often fielded softball and volleyball teams, which were both immensely popular, as was boxing. Basketball was not yet a popular sport. Table tennis (ping-pong) tournaments were common. Pool tables were available in enlisted men's clubs. There were also gymnasiums, movie theaters, playhouses, and libraries on post. The United Service Organization (USO), a non-profit organization, organized events with local live bands and performers, and USO centers sprang up in American towns adjacent to bases. The USO also hosted dances, showed movies, provided free coffee and donuts, and had a recreation room with cards, board games, and other activities.

were a day off with religious services available. For recruits experiencing difficulties in mastering their skills they were often restricted to the barracks and provided remediable training.

The company area was the fiefdom of the company commander. The troops, unless attending training, were restricted to the company area. They required permission to leave the area and had to sign out in the orderly room. After basic training this was relaxed, but a soldier had to at least notify his platoon sergeant he was going to the post exchange (PX), a movie, or so on. They were usually pretty free to come and go at weekends.

The company area contained six to eight buildings. The orderly room held the offices of the CO and first sergeant, and perhaps one for the XO. The orderly room itself was occupied by the company clerk. The back two-thirds of the building was the supply room and within this was the arms room. Next door was the day room, the company's "living room." There were chairs, a few tables, often a ping-pong table, magazine racks, board and card games, and perhaps a modest paperback book library. It was also used as a classroom.

The mess hall contained the kitchen with ovens, stoves, refrigerators, freezer, dough mixer, work tables, sinks, racks for utensils and pots and pans, and a rations storage room. Outside the kitchen was the stainless steel serving line with a steam table. The dining room had six- or eight-man tables with benches. In the back corners were tables for the officers and senior NCOs.

Sometimes there was a storage building for unit equipment where all the field gear was stowed, including pioneer and carpenter tool kits, field ranges, and a great deal of other gear. Sometimes this might be stowed in a battalion stowage building. Because of shortages some mess halls did not initially have stoves and ovens and had to make do with their gasoline-fueled field ranges.

The three or four platoon barracks were aligned behind the one-story administrative buildings. The barracks were two-story buildings with open squad bays on both floors. A squad's double bunks were arrayed on one side of the bay, with a squad on each side. At one end were two one-man rooms for NCOs. Two NCOs might bunk in one room though. A door was set in the barrack's end between these two rooms. At the opposite end was the latrine with sinks and mirrors, toilets, urinals, and a shower room. The barracks was set on foundation blocks, but the latrine was on a ground-level concrete slab. Beside the latrine was the stairwell to the second floor, entered through a side door. Again there was a large squad bay and over the latrine were a one- or two-man room and a larger room for 2–4 NCOs. At the far end was an escape door with a small porch. Here, a ladder allowed access to the ground. There were usually only three company barracks and the company headquarters personnel were split up, with some men in each platoon barracks. They would have one side of a squad bay for example. Double, or in some cases, single bunks were lined up on each side of the bay. Each man had a plywood footlocker at the foot of his bunk, and a laundry bag hung on the bunk with a towel. There was a shelf on the wall for gear, and uniforms were hung beneath it. Some units had wooden or steel wall lockers.

An M3 medium tank crosses an M2 pontoon bridge. Here, a .30-cal. M1919A4 light machine gun on an M1917A1 heavy machine-gun mount is set up for antiaircraft protection. This is probably a substitute for expensive M1917A1 guns. It was found that air defense was best provided by emplacing the guns ashore rather than on the target.

Garrison chow

In garrison the Army served fresh and frozen foods purchased from the local economy. It often proved to be of better quantity than most experienced at home. A commonly heard motto displayed over serving lines was "Take all you want, but eat all you take." Of course, the quality was dependent on the mess section's skill.

Breakfast was typically scrambled or fried eggs (one could have them fried in the manner preferred, called "eggs to order"), bacon or sausage, cereal, toast, hash browns, grits or oatmeal, pancakes, and French toast or the infamous "shit on a shingle" – chipped beef and gravy on toast. There was plenty of coffee, milk, and fruit juice.

Lunch was usually a lighter meal with meat, often cold cuts, two vegetables, bread, and sometimes fruit. Supper was much the same, but with a little more food. Salads were usually served with supper. Meats included beef, pork chops, mutton, ground beef, meat loaf, chicken, hash, stew, and on Fridays there was fish. There were potatoes in some form served at most meals, plus another vegetable such as corn, carrots, different forms of beans (pinto, lima, navy, string, white, etc), peas, squash, and so on. White bread and cornbread were served, as was cake or pie.

Meals were served on stainless steel trays with soldiers going through serving lines. Men on KP duty served the food, except for the meat which only cooks served to prevent KPs giving their buddies extra portions. Some units used ceramic plates and served their meals family-style, that is, platters and bowls were taken to each table and the dishes passed around.

When out on the range or training areas chow was "Mermited" out in insulated food containers and served on mess hall trays rather than mess kits as they were difficult to clean in the field. Dirty trays were returned and cleaned in the mess hall. The same might occur if bivouacked in the field, or the mess section might move to the field and prepare meals in a kitchen tent. This was training for the cooks, but the quality of meals suffered. Seldom were combat-type field rations served during stateside field training. They were needed in combat zones.

Work details and duty

On the newly built posts there were endless work details in order to "finish" and maintain them. Every unit conducted police call picking up litter in its own area, and might be assigned others areas not "belonging" to specific units such as along post roads. "If it didn't grow there, pick it up" was the rule. Details included grass and weed cutting, coal unloading, garbage collection, training area clearing, building simple facilities, warehouse and ammunition supply point unloading details, and all manner of things seemed to need painting. The traditional whitewashing of rocks lining walkways seemed endless. Typically, small work details were placed in charge of a Pfc or corporal, who was strictly a supervisor and did not take part in the work himself.

Post guard duty was an infrequent requirement as it was rotated between units. Guard mount was held daily under the commander of the guard who conducted a very demanding inspection and questioned the guards on the 11 General Orders of the Sentry. Typical guard posts (stood for two hours with four hours off) included motor pools, ammunition supply points, certain supply warehouses, and fuel depots.

At night each company appointed a "charge of quarters" (CQ), a junior NCO, who manned the orderly room all night. If there was an alert the battalion headquarters would notify the CQs who could contact company officers and NCOs. They signed men in returning from pass, ensured lights were out after Taps was played over the post public address system, periodically checked the company area, awakened the NCOs before reveille, answered the phone, and picked up the mail.

Kitchen police duty was more common, perhaps being drawn every two weeks. This usually began at 0330hrs and might go on as late as 2200hrs. The most dreaded job was "pots and pans man." He was responsible for endlessly scrubbing the many pots, pans, and utensils. "Dish washers" cleaned the dining ware and silverware. "Dining room orderlies" (DROs) cleaned the tables and floors after

An M4 medium tank crosses an M2 pontoon-supported treadway bridge, which could support up to 40 tons. The Sherman's 30-ton weight's effect can be seen as it crosses. Typical crossing speed was 5mph to prevent excessive compression effects and minimize wear.

each meal and took care of many other chores including peeling hundreds of potatoes. The most "desirable" job was the "outside man." He manned the loading dock sorting garbage by category into cans, cleaning garbage cans, hosing off the loading dock, and carrying in food deliveries. It was desirable because being outside he was out from under the direct pestering of the "KP pusher."

The gravel crusher was mounted on a six-wheel trailer. Its two conveyer arms allowed two dump trucks to be loaded simultaneously.

APPEARANCE

Uniforms

The issue of uniforms a few days after arriving at the reception center was a high point for the recruits. They now knew they were in the Army, even more so than when they would be issued rifles.

Woolen OD uniforms were everyday wear for field and service use. A lighter OD necktie, peaked round service cap, and an OD woolen garrison cap were worn. For service wear an OD coat was provided. In the field the light green or tan M1941 "Parson's jacket" was worn and the necktie omitted. This was a waist-length, wind-repellant, water-repellent jacket commonly called the "GI jacket." A heavy woolen overcoat was also issued, as was a raincoat. Deployed units usually received ponchos, which were more practical. For summer wear, khaki (light tan) cotton uniforms were issued with a long-sleeve shirt. A khaki garrison cap was provided.

Footwear, whether service shoes or a variety of boots, were russet brown, a reddish shade. Tan canvas lace-up leggings were worn in the field with the trousers bloused into them. Socks were OD in color and most underwear was white. Besides a wide range of climate protective clothing the engineers were also provided special items including knee- or hip-length rubber boots, rain suits, barbed-wire gauntlets, and other types of work gloves.

The Corps of Engineers branch of service insignia was a gold-colored, twin-turreted castle worn on the uniform collars, called "collar brass." Enlisted men's insignia were smaller than officers' and were displayed on a brass disc 1in. in diameter. The branch color was scarlet (commonly called "red") with white as a secondary color. Enlisted men displayed red piping mixed with white threads on garrison caps. Company guidons and battalion colors were also red with white markings and insignia.

A few engineer units were issued the camouflage uniform during the Normandy Campaign, but they were later withdrawn as they caused friendly fire incidents when they were confused with Waffen-SS and Fallschirmjäger troops.

Individual equipment

Combat engineers received the same equipment as infantrymen, called "TA-50 gear," named after Table of Allowance 50. Dark tan-colored web gear (dark OD web gear began to be issued in 1943) consisted of the M1923 dismounted cartridge belt. It had ten pockets each holding two

five-round Springfield loading clips or an eight-round Garand clip. The M1924 first-aid pouch was attached to the bottom of the second clip pocket on the belt's right front. It contained a sardine-like can with a Carlisle field dressing. The M1910 canteen carrier was attached below the fourth cartridge pocket so it would rest over the right hip. A 1qt aluminum or stainless steel canteen went into this along with the nested 1pt canteen cup.

The M1928 haversack was difficult to pack, with integral shoulder straps attaching to the cartridge belt. The haversack could be carried only when the cartridge belt was worn and the complete set of gear had to be removed and five snap-hooks unfastened to remove the pack. This was totally impractical and the pack was inadequate for carrying anything more than the specified "by the book" contents: the shelter-half, blanket, tent pole sections, and stakes. Ration cans and toilet articles were also packed inside and the mess kit carried in an external pocket. There was no room for additional protective clothing or rations. The bayonet was carried on the left side of the pack and the entrenching tool on the back. Both had to be removed and attached to the cartridge belt when going into combat without the pack. Since the pack's shoulder straps doubled as the belt suspenders, when the pack was removed the soldier had to bear the cartridge belt and the attached equipment on his hips.

With the haversack came a triangular pack carrier, into which troops rolled up their overcoat, raincoat or poncho into a U-shaped "horseshoe roll" to carry as part of the pack. The actual items carried depended on the weather. To use any of these the horseshoe roll had to be unrolled, the desired item removed, and it all rolled up again and reattached to the pack. Trying to roll up the pack at 0300hrs in the morning with cold-numbed fingers in the rain on wet and muddy ground was just about impossible.

The M1910 entrenching tool was of the T-handle type and had a fixed blade. Recruits soon learned they could call it an "e-tool," but *never* a "shovel." Not every man carried an e-tool. Within the squad one man carried an M1910 hatchet, two carried an M1910 pick mattock, and one an M1938 wire-cutter. From late 1944 units began to receive the more practical M1944 combat field pack consisting of a backpack and a detachable

Troops move up to the front carrying M1 Bangalore torpedoes and detcord spools. M5 assault gas masks are carried on their chests in black rubber waterproof M7 cases.

cargo pack for additional items. Its suspenders still had to be attached to the belt when carried.

The gas mask and its carrier were worn on the left side with the carrying strap over the right shoulder and a retaining strap around the waist. Much was made of always having the gas mask on hand, at least in training.

Engineer equipment

Regardless of the quantity of mechanized equipment available to US troops, combat engineers relied heavily on hand tools and strong backs. The tools were provided in squad and platoon pioneer and carpenter sets packed in plywood cases. Squads were equipped with the "engineer pioneer equipment squad set No. 1:" with shovels, picks, axes, brush hook, post hole auger, sledgehammer, machetes, jack, and minor tools. The "carpenter equipment squad set No. 1" contained hammers, hatchets, hacksaw, crowbars, maul, handsaws, 1½-man crosscut saw, screwdrivers, level, chisels, and other carpentry tools. The "engineer pioneer equipment combat platoon set No. 3" consisted of heavier hand tools including wreaking bars, mauls, lineman's belt and pole climbers, bench grinder, sledgehammers, pipe wrench, and spare handles for squad tools. The "carpenter equipment

B   **COMBAT ENGINEER FIELD EQUIPMENT**

The "junk on a bunk" display of early war issue equipment is typical of what a combat engineer carried. The late-war equipment would not be much different other than its being the dark green olive drab rather than the tan shade of olive drab. This same type of equipment display would also be exhibited as a "full field layout" on a spread shelter-half or poncho. Often, this was displayed on a poncho before an erected "pup tent."

1. Spare fatigue shirt and trousers.
2. Shelter-half and woolen blanket.
3. Tent stakes (x5).
4. Tent pole sections (x3).
5. Tent guy-rope.
6. Spare long underwear shirt and drawers.
7. Spare handkerchief.
8. M1910 canteen carrier.
9. M1924 first aid pouch with Carlisle dressing.
10. M1923 cartridge belt.
11. M1910 mess kit with M1926 utensils.
12. M1928 haversack.
13. Toilet articles on towel.
14. M1910 1qt canteen and canteen cup.
15. .30-cal. M1903 rifle.
16. M1905 bayonet and scabbard.
17. M4 gas mask and M6 carrier.
18. M1 steel helmet and liner.
19. Engineer pocketknife.

The combat engineer soldier wears the typical 1944 combat uniform with M1941 "Parson jacket," woolen shirt and trousers, service shoes with leggings, the newer dark olive drab web gear, and a .30-cal. M1 rifle.

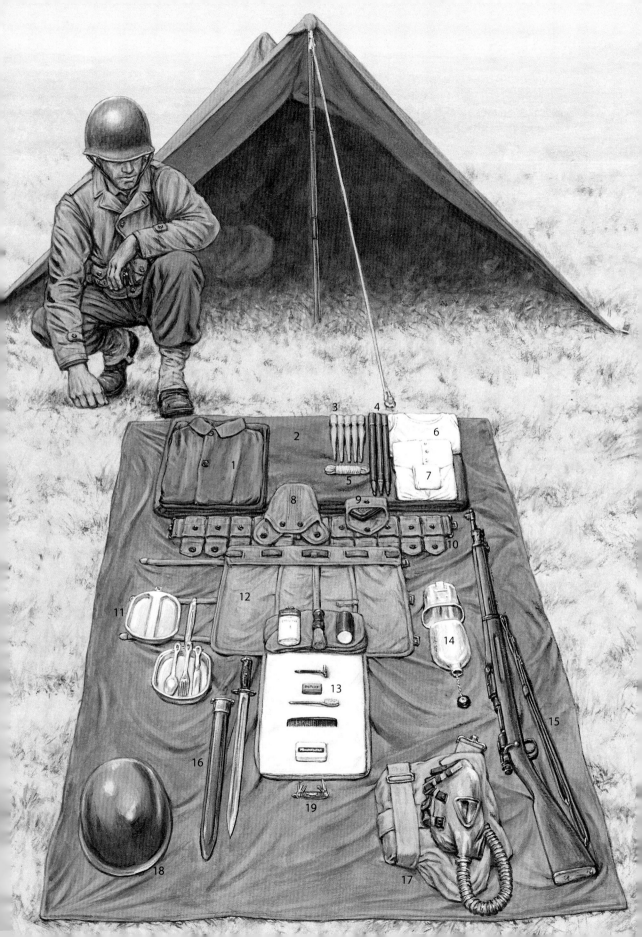

platoon set No. 3" contained more specialized tools plus additional common woodworking tools.

A key piece of equipment was the Mall Tool Company Model 6 chainsaw, issued on a basis of one per platoon. It was powered by a 5hp two-cycle gasoline engine with a 36in. blade. It required two men to operate the heavy machine and had a handle on the end of the blade for the assistant.

Pneumatic jackhammers were also used. In the battalion there was one pneumatic drill and tamper to drill boreholes for demolitions and to compact soil such as roadbeds and foundations. Other items used by engineers included M13 binoculars, lensatic compasses, TL-122 flashlights, M1 mine probes, and radioactive luminous markers to identify lanes and gaps through minefields and obstacles.

Engineers were taught how to efficiently use block and tackle, ropes, and tow chains, and how to set up A-frames to move or displace heavy items such as obstacles, logs, boulders, etc. Each squad's dump truck had a 10,000lb capacity winch on the front. Its cable could be connected to a block and tackle system for motive power.

Demolition was a key part of the engineers' capabilities. The "engineer demolition squad set No. 1" contained a ten-cap blasting machine, cap crimper, wire-cutter, detonating cord drill, galvanometer for testing

Some of the combat engineers' most important equipment: demolitions. To the left are ½lb TNT blocks and to the right are M2 chain demolition blocks linked by detonating cord. In the foreground are various types of electric and non-electric blasting caps, timed fuses, and M1 fuse igniters.

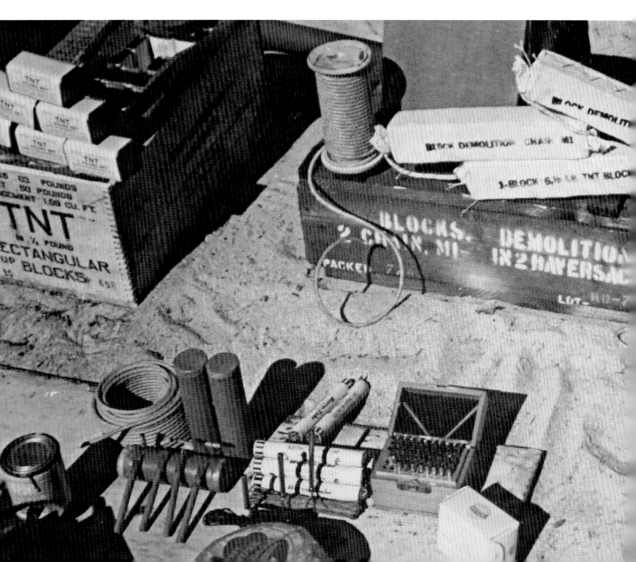

electrical circuits, friction tape, copper wire, twine, and 500ft wire reel, plus quantities of electric and non-electric blasting caps, detonating cord, time delay fuse, fuse lighters, and TNT charges. The "engineer demolition platoon set No. 2" contained more of the same, but larger quantities of demolition charges, caps, and related material. Demolition charges could be used individually or taped together in the necessary quantities.

Engineer light equipment companies and construction battalions provided heavier construction equipment in the form of angle-dozers, motorized air compressors, road graders, road rollers, 4-ton dump trucks, concrete mixers, motorized earth augers, powered shovels, clamshell crane trucks, sawmills, and gravel crushers.

Weapons

Combat engineers used basically the same weapons as the infantry, but not in all cases. The basic individual weapon was the rifle. While many American boys had fired deer rifles, .22 hunting rifles, and shotguns, most, especially from the cities, had not. There is a big difference between combat firing techniques with a high-powered semi-automatic rifle and civilian hunting firearms. Even experienced hunters found they had much to learn, although they did have an edge on their inexperienced counterparts.

In training, especially prior to 1943, many units were issued the old standby Springfield .30-cal. M1903 or M1903A1 rifle. The Springfield was bolt-action and fed by a five-round magazine. Once a unit was identified for overseas deployment it would receive the Garand .30-cal. M1 rifle, although units raised from 1943 on often received Garands straight off. The M1 proved to be one of the best rifles of World War II and its ruggedness is little disputed. Nor is the fact that its semi-automatic firepower and rapidly reloaded eight-round magazine was a significant factor in close-range engagements. A Garand-armed rifleman could fire 15–18 aimed shots a minute as opposed to a Mauser-armed German only getting off 10 shots. It was a heavy weapon, weighing 9.5lb when empty. The gas-operated M1 rifle did have more parts than the Springfield though, and required more cleaning time. The 16in. M1905 or M1942 bayonet

Standard US demolition charges

1lb nitrostarch charge
½lb TNT charge
1lb TNT charge
20lb M1 tetrytol charge (eight 2½lb blocks linked with detcord)
20lb M2 tetrytol charge (eight 2½lb blocks without detcord)
½lb Composition C charge
2½lb Composition C charge
2½lb M3 C2 plastic charge
½lb M4 C2 plastic charge
13lb M1 Bangalore torpedo
13lb M1 and M2 shaped charges
15lb M2A3 shaped charge
45lb M3 shaped charge
40lb ammonium nitrate cratering charge

See Osprey Elite 160, *World War II Infantry Assault Tactics* for descriptions.

The SCR-625 mine detector

The "outdoor carpet sweeper" or "detector set, mine, SCR-625" (SCR stood for Signal Corps Radio) proved to be quite effective when it saw its first use in North Africa in late 1942. Developed by the Hazeltine Company, it consisted of a telescoping 6ft handle, to which a wooden 18in.-diameter disc-shaped head (metal-covered on top and around the edges) was attached to its underside along with a wedge-shaped search coil. The detector weighed 7.5lb in addition to a 7lb amplifier haversack, together with the battery that induced a magnetic field in the search coil. The operator slowly walked forwards, sweeping the search head in a 3–4ft arc several inches off the ground. He could hear a faint buzzing tone in his earphones. When he swept over a buried metallic object the buzz immediately increased in pitch and could be quite shrill. Once a suspected mine was detected the operator slowly swung the search head in decreasingly smaller arcs watching a meter on the handle. The meter's needle showed the strongest magnetic reading coupled with the highest pitch tone to closely narrow down the mine's location, at a depth of up to 12in. below the ground.

The $491 SCR-625 had its flaws. It was considered too heavy for prolonged sweeping and that, coupled with the unrelenting tone in one's ears and having to walk slowly upright through a minefield, which might contain non-metallic mines and tripwire-activated mines and booby traps, meant operators had to be relieved frequently. It was not waterproof and rather fragile. In the Italian theater the mine detector was found to be less effective. There was more iron in European soil and the Germans were increasingly employing non-metallic mines made of wood, glass, or ceramics with very few small metal components. Even though improved versions, the last being the SCR-625-E, were developed with increased sensitivity to detect smaller metal components, this did not really improve its ability to detect non-metallic mines because it increased the interference in iron-rich soil and also picked up the more numerous shell fragments, nails, discarded tins, and other bits of miscellaneous metal. The Germans also buried scrap metal within minefields to hamper mine detectors, and detectors were impossible to use along railroad tracks.

was issued together with the M1 rifle. From 1943, 10in. M1905E1 and M1 bayonets were issued, which were handier in close quarters.

While most members of an engineer company were armed with M1 rifles, officers and staff sergeants and up were armed with the .30-cal. M1 carbine. It used a much smaller round than M1 rifles and machine guns. The 5.5lb carbine used a 15-round detachable magazine.

Engineer squads were issued the M7 grenade launcher for use with the M1 rifle, and the platoon headquarters had an M8 grenade launcher for the M1 carbine, while the company headquarters had three M8s. These could launch colored smoke and flare signals, and M9A1 antitank, M17 fragmentation, and M19 white phosphorus grenades. There were adaptors to which "pineapple" fragmentation and colored smoke hand grenades could be fitted and fired from grenade launchers.

Hand grenades included Mk II and Mk IIA1 "pineapple" fragmentation, Mk IIIA1 offensive "concussion," AN-M8 white smoke for screening, AN-M14 thermite incendiary for destroying enemy equipment and one's own equipment to prevent its use by the enemy, and M15 WP (white phosphorus), which could be used for screening and could also cause casualties.

In most armies flame-throwers were assigned to the engineers. Assault engineer teams with flame-throwers and demolitions were attached to infantry units to reinforce their assault capabilities. The US combat engineers were no different initially. A combat engineer battalion was authorized 24 flame-throwers, which were assigned to the headquarters company's supply section. Often they simply remained in depot as they were little used in the Mediterranean and European theaters. In March 1944 (prior to the Normandy landings) they were withdrawn from engineer battalions, but were still available for issue from depots. They could be issued to engineer or infantry units.

The M1A1 portable flame-thrower weighed 70lb with four gallons of gasoline. Its range was about 50yds when using thickened fuel and

C   ENGINEER DEMOLITIONS TRAINING

The engineer battalion cadre staff sergeant prepares a display of demolition materials. The staff sergeant wears the mackinaw coat, woolen trousers, and rubber boots over his service shoes and leggings. The 1lb nitrostarch charge (**1**) was later replaced by TNT charges, as it was dangerously unstable. The ½lb TNT charge (**2**) was one of the most widely used charges throughout the war; it was later produced with olive drab covers. The 1lb TNT charge (**3**) was introduced in 1943; the early charge had yellow covers. The 2½lb M2 tetrytol demolition block is shown at (**4**). The 2¼lb M3 composition C2 or C3 demolition block (**5**) was a plastic explosive. The M1 demolition charge haversack (**6**) contained eight 2½lb M1 tetrytol changes (similar to M2 charges) linked together by detcord. The M2 and M3 charges were carried in the same 22lb satchel charge. The 10lb M1 shaped-charge (**7**) with folding legs could penetrate 12in. of armor and 36in. of concrete. Detonating cord spool, 100ft (**8**) was used to link together demolition charges for simultaneous detonation. Detcord was not a timed safety fuse. The 40lb M3 shaped-charge (**9**) with detachable legs could punch through 60in. of concrete. The ammonium nitrate 40lb cratering charge (**10**) was used to blast large craters in roads and runways and blow apart obstacles. When used for cratering they first were lowered into a borehole. The pole charge (**11**) was fabricated in the field. This one has 20 ½lb TNT charges detonated by two lengths of detcord running up the handle, with 3in. of white safety fuse with blasting caps taped to the end of the detcord, activated by M1 fuse igniters attached to a few inches of safety fuse. The pole allowed the attacker to shove it into a pillbox embrasure without exposing himself to the field of fire. The M1 Bangalore torpedo (**12**) was 5ft long and contained 9lb of amatol. Used for breaching wire obstacles and minefields, they could be attached end-to-end up to a length of 200ft. Several could be bundled together for use against denser barriers.

The M1A1 flame-thrower was a terrifying weapon. It saw little use in Europe when compared with its use in the Pacific theater. It could fire four or five two-second bursts up to 40yds.

40yds without. The M2-2 flame-thrower of 1944 added about 10yds to the range and was more reliable. Thickened fuel was achieved by adding napalm powder. Contrary to the image portrayed in movies, it is almost impossible to cause the flame-thrower to explode by hitting it with bullets or explosive fragments.

CONDITIONS OF SERVICE

On stateside posts most quarters were adequate and for the most part brand new. The Corps of Engineers designed scores of "temporary" wooden-frame buildings for military posts. These were built either by civilian contractors or engineer construction battalions as part of their training. These included post and unit headquarters, administrative buildings of all sorts, warehouses, storage buildings, supply facilities, laundries, medical and dental clinics, hospitals, PXs, quartermaster sales buildings, bachelor officers' quarters (BOQ), movie theaters, playhouses, gymnasiums, libraries, chapels, classrooms; enlisted, NCO and officer clubs; mess halls, barracks, day rooms, supply rooms, maintenance facilities, workshops, motor pools, garages, post stockades (military jails), military police stations, and generally every type of facility needed to support a garrison.

These one- and two-story structures were mostly built of wooden planks with composite shingle roofs and set on concrete block foundations. Some were built on concrete slabs. They were heated with coal furnaces and stoves. Except for higher headquarters buildings, most were unfinished inside – there was no paneling or sheetrock on interior walls (or insulation), and they were unpainted. They were provided with good electrical lighting, sufficient screen-covered windows for natural light and ventilation, indoor latrines, and hot and cold running water. Water treatment and sewage treatment facilities were built and the local civilian power grid expanded to accommodate the new military posts.

These "temporary" buildings remained the mainstay of structures on posts well into the 1970s, when they gradually began to be replaced by modern buildings. Almost 70 years after they were built some can still be found on posts, much updated, in secondary roles and awaiting replacement.

A second form of structure was also built and was meant to be even more temporary. These were wooden-framed buildings walled only by tarpaper, with plywood floors set on concrete blocks. Theaters, chapels, and headquarters buildings were often built amongst these, with the intent of replacing the tarpaper hutments with wooden buildings at a later date.

A third form of quarters was the "tent city." Units would live beneath canvas with all necessary facilities set up under field conditions. This included kitchens, showers, washrooms, and temporary latrine pits. Eventually, wooden-frame quarters would become available and they would move to a more amenable abode. Units undertaking field training or participating in prolonged maneuvers might also live in tent cities. Life under canvas had its advantages. There was not as much "spic and span" or clean-up required and it could be pleasant in mild weather. Nevertheless, in adverse weather it could be quite miserable. Coal and oil-fired stoves were available, but the drafty un-insulated tents were cold nonetheless.

The troops also saw a great deal of the training areas and ranges where they spent many of their waking hours. The post's facilities and troop quarters were usually in a single area near the post's main entrance and were collectively known as the cantonment area. Everything else on the sprawling military posts consisted of training areas, firing ranges, and impact areas around which the various ranges were situated.

Liberty was granted for 24 or 48 hours at a time; seldom was a 72- or 96-hour liberty given. In peacetime a soldier was authorized 30 days' paid leave a year. This

Engineers prepare to place an entire case of ½lb TNT blocks inside a PzKpfw IV tank. This would not only blow the turret off, but would blast apart most of the hull.

was greatly restricted in wartime. Leave was granted in the US occasionally, but usually to entire units prior to deployment rather than to individuals. This might be only for a week or so. Individuals being reassigned to another post were sometimes allowed a delay in travel as a form of leave so they could visit home. Any remaining leave, and this was often a considerable amount at the time of discharge, was either paid off or the individual was allowed to go home early and continued to receive pay for the remaining leave time.

Payday was the last Friday of the month, sometimes resulting in a "payday weekend." This meant a two-day pass with Friday afternoon off and the troops reporting back on Sunday evening. There was often an inspection prior to pay formation. This might be an individual inspection in formation, but usually included a quarters inspection. Any infractions might mean restriction to post.

Pay call was held after a company formation when roll call was taken. It might be held outdoors on a field desk, but was usually held in the mess hall or day room, especially in poor weather. The company commander sat at a desk armed with a loaded .45-cal. pistol required by regulations. The XO and first sergeant were present and called off the names in alphabetical order. When called each soldier stepped up to the desk, saluted, and reported with his name and serial number presenting his ID card. The CO counted out the money the soldier had coming according to a list furnished by the unit's higher headquarters' finance section. The soldier accepted the money, saluted, stepped back, and departed. The CO did not return salutes during pay call in order not to be distracted.

Besides base pay there were allotments for married soldiers and those with children. Foreign Service Pay was 20 percent of base pay (e.g. $10 for a private under grade three). Enlisted men presented with the Silver Star, Distinguished Service Medal, or Medal of Honor received $2 a month for each decoration. There was no combat pay in World War II.

Automatic payroll deductions could be made to a soldier's wife or parents. For wives and unemployed parents or a widowed parent the government matched the deduction. Soldiers paid $6.40 a month for National Serviceman's Life Insurance. If killed while in the service, combat-related or not, the soldier's beneficiary received $10,000. They also received six months' base pay. This was a considerable sum in the 1940s and led to the coining of the phrase "bought the farm" as a deceased soldier's family could very well pay off what they owed on their farm.

What money a soldier had left over after allotments to his wife or parents he spent on laundry, shoe polish, cigarettes, toothpaste, stationery, postage

D **THE BARRACKS**

Wall lockers were seldom available, and uniforms were hung beneath a shelf instead. Individual equipment was stowed on the shelf. Here, this cannot be seen as it is being worn by the soldier for an outdoor equipment inspection. It could also be displayed on the bunk for inspection, called "junk on a bunk." Normally the second blanket, rather than being folded beneath the pillow, covered the pillow and was tucked in under the mattress and known as the "dust cover." One day a week they would leave their bunks unmade with the sheets loosely piled atop the blanket to air out. Linen would be exchanged once a week. The barracks bag tied to the head of the bunk was for dirty laundry. The plywood footlocker's main compartment contained (from left the right) tightly rolled woolen undershirts, woolen underdrawers, cotton undershirts, and cotton underdrawers. The tray held socks, toilet articles, shoeshine and cleaning materials, and the few authorized personal effects. No civilian clothes were permitted.

US Army enlisted rank and pay – 1942–48

Rank	Abbrev.	Pay grade
Private	Pvt.	7
Private first class	Pfc.	6
Technician 5th grade	Tech. 5 or T/5	5
Corporal	Cpl.	5
Technician 4th grade	Tech. 4 or T/4	4
Sergeant	Sgt.	4
Technician 3rd grade	Tech. 3 or T/3	3
Staff sergeant	S/Sgt.	3
Technical sergeant	T/Sgt.	2
First sergeant	1st Sgt.	1
Master sergeant	M/Sgt.	1

Prior to January 1942 there were no technicians 5, 4, or 3.
Prior to September 1942 first sergeants were at pay grade 2.

The below base pay increased every three years. Most soldiers, regardless of rank, and, unless they had been in the Regular Army or National Guard prior to the war and had more years, were receiving over three years' pay by the time of the Normandy invasion.

Pay grade	Base pay	
	Less than 3 years	Over 3 years
7	$50.00	$52.50
6	$54.00	$56.70
5	$66.00	$69.30
4	$78.00	$81.90
3	$96.00	$100.80
2	$114.00	$119.70
1	$138.00	$144.90

For comparison purposes, a 2nd lieutenant platoon leader with less than three years' of service made $150 a month.

stamps, toilet articles, other necessities, and the occasional soft drink, beer and candy bar or visit to the post theater. Many simply stayed on post visiting the beer garden, movie theaters, enlisted clubs, or the off-base United Service Organization (USO) club for free entertainment and snacks.

Popular off-post entertainment included bars, nightclubs, dancehalls, boxing matches, and movies. Local communities often arranged dances for GIs to which girls flocked for their own entertainment, and in some cases, hopes of finding a husband. These "GI hops" were held in National Guard armories, community centers, or on post. Some girls, "Allotment Annies," married unsuspecting soldiers to benefit from the allotment check. When the soldier moved on the girl found another husband. There were girls with up to six "husbands" making a good living off the checks they received. A lesser threat were "B-girls" (bar girls), bar and club hostesses who encouraged servicemen to drink more and to buy them drinks. They received a small commission from each drink sold. Girls were also motivated for patriotic reasons. They felt it their "duty" to do something for the boys in uniform. Professional prostitutes ("street-walkers") and amateurs ("victory girls") were available at $3–$10. The amateur prostitutes or promiscuous girls, often teenagers, were also known as "V-girls," "good-time girls," "pick-up girls," "khaki wackies," "cuddle bunnies," "patriotutes," and "chippies." Caught up in the excitement and patriotic fervor of the times, some did not solicit money, but were simply sympathetic to young men going overseas to possible death.

Contracting venereal disease was a chargeable offense. It was the soldier's responsibility to use condoms and visit a prophylaxis-station ("pro-station") or use a "pro-kit" after his "date." It was manned by a medical officer

on or near posts where servicemen were required to report for VD preventive treatment when returning from pass. "Short arm" inspections were conducted with the troops falling out wearing only raincoats and jock straps for inspection by medical personnel. A toilet stall in the latrine was reserved for those who contracted VD. The Army Good Conduct Medal was awarded for maintaining a clean record during a three-year enlistment. Contracting VD denied the award of the "No-Clap Medal."

A British-designed Bailey bridge replaces a destroyed masonry bridge using some of the original piers and abutments for support. The damaged portions of these would be cleared down to what was still solid and then timber supports built.

ON CAMPAIGN

The combat engineer battalion

The divisional combat engineer battalion was assigned a wide range of tasks, including:

> Engineer reconnaissance of routes, bridges, river-crossing sites, bivouac sites, etc.
> Building, maintaining, and repairing roads, trails, bridges, and culverts.
> Installing and maintaining portable tactical bridges.
> Clearing light aircraft landing strips.
> Constructing simple structures.
> Providing demolitions support.
> Breaching and clearing obstacles, roadblocks, and debris.
> Clearing minefields, booby traps, and dud munitions.
> Operating water supply points.
> Issuing engineer supplies and materials to other divisional units.
> Providing technical assistance and advice to other units on the construction and layout of fortifications, obstacles, camouflage, and minefields.
> Reinforcing infantry assault units with demolition specialists, obstacle-breaching specialists, and flame-thrower operators.

BELOW
Some units added armor plate to D7 Cats to allow them to operate under small-arms fire. This is one of several variants. Note that the driver's cab is open-topped.

BELOW RIGHT
The Diamond T Motor Company's 4-ton truck was specifically designed for the Corps of Engineers. Besides this Model 968A cargo truck version used to tow construction equipment trailers there was also a 4-ton dump truck. It has a 15,000lb winch on the front bumper.

Prior to August 8, 1944 an engineer battalion had a strength of 31 commissioned officers, three warrant officers, and 649 enlisted men. On that date the strength was reduced to 605 enlisted men with no change in officer strength. The reduction was achieved by eliminating small numbers of administrative and service personnel and a number of basic privates from the company headquarters. Basic privates were those who had completed only basic training and were not trained in specific skills. They assisted headquarters personnel and served as fillers. In combat, the eight basic private slots in an engineer company headquarters were usually vacant. The engineer platoons lost only one man from the headquarters, the weapons sergeant, who had been responsible for the machine guns. The study of unit rosters shows that some units retained the position, at least for a time, perhaps in lieu of the 2½-ton truck driver. While a number of slots were lost in the battalion, several radio operators were added to the companies to improve tactical communications,

but most radios were removed. There were no backpack or hand-held radios available.

The battalion headquarters and the headquarters and service company (HHSC) consisted of the battalion headquarters with ten officers, an element separate from but related to the headquarters and service company. The headquarters and service company was organized into the company headquarters with one officer (the CO, a captain) and 16 enlisted men. The division engineer section had three enlisted men. The lieutenant-colonel CO and his staff doubled as the division engineer staff, and part of the staff spent much of their time at the division headquarters. The administrative section had one warrant officer and 18 enlisted men. The five-man intelligence section supported the S-2 and the eight-man operations section backed the S-3. The six-man reconnaissance section worked for the S-2. It possessed two jeeps each manned by an NCO and two radio operators under the staff reconnaissance officer. Their job was to reconnoiter routes and worksites. The supply section had a warrant officer and 30 enlisted men. It possessed nine 2½-ton trucks plus a ¾-ton weapons carrier and seven trailers. These vehicles carried an air compressor, mines, demolitions, and water, plus 14 M2 assault boats and six two-man pneumatic boats. The maintenance section with one warrant officer and 18 enlisted men repaired and maintained the battalion's vehicles and powered engineer equipment. It possessed a ¾-ton weapons carrier, 2½-ton cargo truck, 4-ton Diamond T wrecker, cargo trailer, and welder trailer. Total HHSC strength was 12 officers, three warrant officers, and 106 enlisted men. The medical detachment had a battalion aid station with two officers and nine enlisted men, with a 1½-ton cargo truck and trailer and a company aid section with six men, two detailed to each company.

The three engineer combat companies had five officers and 162 enlisted men. The company headquarters was organized into the command group with the CO (a captain) and 19 enlisted men (first sergeant, clerk, bugler, three mechanics, three radio operators, carpenter, air compressor operator, and eight basic privates), plus the administration group with a lieutenant acting as mess, supply, and transportation officer (effectively the XO, although not designated as such) and 14 enlisted men

ABOVE LEFT
A Dodge ½-ton WC-21 weapons carrier mounting a .30-cal. M1917A1 heavy machine gun being employed during maneuvers. This began to be replaced by the Dodge ¾-ton WC-51 weapons carrier in early 1942. Two such vehicles were assigned to engineer company headquarters. Note the .30-cal. M1903 Springfield rifle used by many units during training.

ABOVE
A Caterpillar D7 dozer tractor, known to the Army as the M1 heavy tractor, was commonly called a D7 or "Cat" by the troops. Here, the winch cable used to operate the dozer blade has been detached and re-rigged to allow the winch to operate a hoisting A-frame.

(mess, supply and motor sergeants; clerk, five cooks, dozer driver, and four drivers).

The company possessed motorized equipment in the form of a jeep, two ¾-ton weapons carriers (one for the CO and one for tools and maintenance gear), a 2½-ton cargo truck with a 1-ton trailer for mess gear and water, and a 4-ton truck with an 8-ton and later a 20-ton Rogers low bed semi-trailer for the M1 heavy tractor (Caterpillar D7 7M or D7 3T bulldozer). There was also an air compressor mounted in the winch-equipped Diamond T 4-ton cargo truck. These 4-tonners were designed specifically for the Corps of Engineers.

The three engineer platoons had on paper an unusual organization. There was a five-man platoon headquarters with a lieutenant platoon commander, staff sergeant platoon sergeant, tech. 5 tool room keeper, tech. 5 truck driver for the jeep, and a private/Pfc. truck driver for the 2½-ton cargo truck mounting a .50-cal. machine gun. The platoon commander and sergeant were armed with carbines (one with a grenade launcher), the jeep driver with a submachine gun, and the other men with rifles. Equipment and tools included a "No. 3 carpenter equipment set," "No. 3 pioneer equipment set," "No. 2 demolition equipment set," and a mine detector. Two .30-cal. M1917A1 water-cooled machine guns were also carried. The rifle-armed weapons sergeant, if retained, supervised the machine guns.

On paper the rest of the platoon was organized into a 39-man "engineer section" composed of three "operating units." The section was superfluous as there was no section leader and no need for a single distinct operating element under a platoon headquarters. It was simply ignored in practice and the three 13-man "operating units" were generally known as "engineer squads." The terms "engineer section" and "operating unit" are not seen in unit histories and memoirs. The typical engineer squad was made up of the following:

Unit [squad] foreman	Sgt.
Asst Unit [squad] foreman	Cpl.
Bridge carpenter	Tech. 4 or 5
General carpenter	Tech. 4 or 5 (x2)
Electrician	Tech. 5 or Pfc./Pvt.
Light truck driver	Tech. 5 or Pfc./Pvt.
Demolition man	Pfc./Pvt.
Jackhammer operator	Pfc./Pvt.
Utility repairman	Pfc./Pvt. (x2)
General rigger	Pfc./Pvt. (x2)

The engineer squad had a 2½-ton dump truck, which transported the squad and its equipment: the "No. 1 carpenter equipment set," "No. 1 pioneer equipment set," "No. 1 demolition equipment set," and an M1 mine probe. All men were armed with M1 riles, and the squad was also equipped with an M7 grenade launcher and a bazooka.

The engineer battalion did not possess a great deal of heavy equipment other than one bulldozer and nine dump trucks per company, with no means of loading dirt into them. To conduct any heavy construction and earthmoving it was necessary for the battalion to be augmented from the corps' engineer combat group. A group typically had two to four combat engineer battalions, a dump truck company, and a light equipment

The 2½-ton GMC dump truck

The engineer squad's 16,850lb dump truck was their primary means of transportation for personnel and equipment. The dump truck was built on the standard General Motors Company CCKW-352H short-wheelbase chassis, the same as used for the famous 2½-ton ("deuce and a half") CCKW-352A cargo truck (equipping engineer platoon headquarters) and many other specialized vehicles. Its 40-gallon gasoline tank provided it with a 220-mile range. Powered by a GMC ("Jimmy") 270-cubic inch straight six-cylinder, 94-horsepower engine, it could reach a speed of 45mph. It had a five-speed transmission and could provide power to all six wheels, leading to its being called a 6 x 6. There were dual tires on the two rear axles. While designated as a 2½-ton truck, that was its off-road cargo capacity. On hard-surface roads it could carry 5 tons. The dump truck version had a 2½-cubic yard capacity tilt bed with an adjustable cab protector and a double-acting tailgate that could hinge at the bottom as in a normal cargo truck, or at the top to serve as a spreader when dumping its load. In order for it to double as an engineer transport it was fitted with removal sideboard slats, folding troop benches (seven men to a side), a front equipment rack, and four bows and a canvas tarp as a cargo bed cover. When rigged in this manner it appeared similar to a normal cargo truck. On the front bumper was a 10,000lb-capacity GarWood or Heil winch with a ½in., 200ft cable.

Early models had hardtop, enclosed cabs, but from mid-1943 they were produced with an "open cab" with a canvas top and canvas side curtain doors.

The GMC 2½-ton CCKW-352H dump truck was standard equipment, with every combat engineer squad possessing one to transport its personnel and equipment. This pre-1943 version with a hardtop lacks the cab protector plate on the front end of the dump bed.

company, which included a pool of construction equipment, plus depot, maintenance, topographic, water supply, and several types of bridge companies. Bridge companies transported bridging materials and equipment, but relied on engineer battalions to provide most of the manpower to erect them. The bridge company provided the technical expertise. At army level there were more of the same types of units plus up to three engineer construction battalions with heavy equipment and more specialized engineer battalions and companies such as camouflage and heavier bridge units.

In combat the divisional engineer battalion operated in the front lines and immediately behind them, supporting the infantry regiments. The most frequent jobs were mine and booby-trap clearance, obstacle breaching, erecting hasty bridges, operating ferries, repairing damaged existing bridges, route reconnaissance, and maintaining supply routes and other roads.

Divisional engineers did not perform engineer work directly for infantry regiments. They did not dig fighting or weapons positions, lay mines, install barbed-wire or other obstacles, or erect camouflage. The infantry did this work themselves with the engineers delivering the materials and providing technical expertise. The engineers had their own work to do. They

 HEAVY EQUIPMENT

Each combat engineer company possessed an M1 heavy tractor – a Caterpillar D7 7M or D7 3T bulldozer. To move this monstrosity about they were provided a White Motor Company Model 666 6-ton cargo truck towing a Rogers 20-ton low bed semi-trailer. The truck mounted a GarWood 25,000lb capstan winch behind the cab. The "Cat" or "dozer" had a rear-mounted Hyster 30,000lb winch, which operated the blade via the overhead gantry rather than hydraulic arms as on modern dozers. The winch cable could be detached from the blade and used for other purposes. Some engineer companies were provided with additional dozers. Each engineer squad had a 2½-ton GMC dump truck with a 10,000lb capacity GarWood or Heil winch. This one had the "open cab," produced since mid-1943. The "dumps" were sometimes concentrated under platoon or company control to haul construction materials such as logs (for bridges, corduroy roads, or obstacle construction), gravel and rock (for road surfacing), barbed-wire coils, and bridge components.

would often set up sawmills to cut timbers and planks en masse for infantry bunkers, bridges, and corduroy roads.

An infantry battalion had its own ammunition and pioneer platoon to deliver ammunition to the front line, lay mines, string barbed wire, and undertake light construction and demolition work. The infantry regiment also had an antitank mine platoon, which could lay and recover antitank and antipersonnel mines and breach enemy minefields, as it possessed mine detectors and probes. The men manning these platoons were specially trained infantrymen.

Additionally, another engineer battalion would be attached to committed divisions from the corps' engineer group. As the division advanced, the attached battalion would take over route maintenance from the divisional battalion to ensure roads and bridges remained usable under the heavy traffic, and would make improvements such as establishing drainage and emplacing heavier-duty bridges. They also recovered and destroyed abandoned enemy equipment and munitions along with the remainder of breached minefields and obstacles. As the division advanced farther these rear areas would be taken over by corps and army engineer units for further upgrades and maintenance.

Engineers as ad hoc infantry

While the engineer battalion could be employed in an infantry role, there were limitations to the missions it could accomplish. It occurred only when necessary, in order to hold gaps when divisions were forced to defend extended frontages, secure exposed flanks, secure rear areas and lines of communication from infiltrators, and mop up after the infantry. The engineers were armed, motorized, and trained to a degree for this mission. It must be stressed though that they lacked the firepower of an infantry battalion and possessed nowhere near the tactical proficiency of an infantry unit. For this reason they were seldom if ever assigned to offensive operations. In emergencies, during the Battle of the Bulge for example, they were sometimes the only units available to defend gaps and exposed flanks. At other times they were forced to mount their own limited attacks to secure worksites.

Besides tactical proficiency the main drawback of employing engineers as infantry was their moderate firepower. There were no 60mm or 81mm mortars. Each engineer platoon had two .30-cal. water-cooled machine guns plus a single

.50-cal., which were incorporated into the defense. The manual prescribed that the company's six water-cooled guns be organized into a machine-gun platoon manned by men drawn from the engineer squads and company headquarters. In reality the guns more likely remained with their platoons, especially since they possessed no BARs.

While each platoon possessed three bazookas, there were no 57mm antitank guns available from the battalion antitank platoon or regimental antitank company, which the infantry benefited from. Nor was there a regimental cannon company with 75mm or 105mm howitzers for fire support.

There were no units from which mortars and other supporting weapons could be detached to reinforce the engineers; the infantry would retain their own. Possibly, towed or self-propelled antitank guns might be attached from the tank destroyer battalion typically attached to each infantry division, but they were often needed to support the main effort making it rare the engineers benefited from them.

Total engineer company armament in 1944/45 was: 151 M1 rifles, 24 M1 carbines, four M1 submachine guns, six .30-cal. M1917A1 machine guns, three .50-cal. M2 machine guns, 12 M7 and six M8 grenade launchers, and nine 2.36in. M9 bazookas.

Another problem was communications. The engineers did not possess as near as robust a system as the infantry and this made command and control more difficult in a unit less than proficient in infantry tactics. They had to be augmented with both radios and field telephones, but spares were seldom available.

It typically required some 24 hours for an engineer battalion to reorganize for an infantry role, establish communications, draw additional ammunition and munitions, and otherwise prepare. Unneeded engineer equipment was stowed in the rear under the care of a rear detachment. Then the battalion had to move into position and, since most missions were defensive, prepare positions. Here they were at an advantage since they were experienced in laying mines, erecting obstacles, and preparing defensive positions and camouflage. Command posts, communications centers, aid stations, ammunition supply points, and reserve supply points had to be established and coordination made with adjacent units and the controlling headquarters. This included integration into the fire control net with artillery forward observers.

The engineers saw their most widespread employment as infantry in the Ardennes at the end of 1944. Numerous battalions, and often entire engineer groups were employed as infantry, mainly in the defense. Many infantry units were shattered and scattered, but most engineer units, being in the rear, were intact and were rushed to the crumbling front to fill gaps, secure flanks, and occupy frontline positions. Some were understrength themselves, but the degree of teamwork they had developed as engineers proved invaluable in the defensive missions.

Life in the field

Since engineers were seldom directly in the front line, they would take advantage of any available structure for shelter: barns, sheds, houses, warehouses, apartments, schools, hotels, and whatever they could find that the infantry had not beaten them to. In Europe, cold nights begin in September and last into May, with November through March being quite severe, often with rain and snow.

Often there was no choice but to bivouac outdoors. In poor weather the engineers tried to locate behind hills, ridges, and woods for wind protection. If near the front line then tree stands were avoided owing to the danger of tree-bursting artillery rounds. If among trees, overhead cover was necessary. They did not always have a free choice of where to bivouac owing to the positions occupied by reserve units immediately behind the front, supply dumps, and artillery units, which had priority for selecting positions. In fact they would give artillery units a wide berth because they drew fire and were noisy. They often had to bivouac at their worksites and these were not always ideal locations.

In cool weather they learned that sleeping in their dump truck's steel bed was colder than the ground. The truck's canvas cover could be fastened to its side and the other edge staked to the ground to form a lean-to shelter. Sleeping under the truck was unsafe and usually forbidden. Two-man pup tents were often used, where two shelter-halves were buttoned together and erected. If possible hay, pine and fir needles, or leaves were laid on the floor for insulation from the cold and damp. One of the men's rubberized ponchos would be laid as a floor. In rainy weather the tent was "trenched," that is, a small trench was dug around it and the dirt piled on the tent's skirt to help keep out water seepage. Regardless, in heavy rains a wet night was expected. Near the front a two-man prone foxhole was dug and the tent erected over it. The depth depended on whether the ground was frozen, the height of the water table, and the presence of rocks and roots.

Officially, two M1934 woolen blankets were issued to each man, but this was inadequate in the European winter. Additional blankets might be issued and supplemented with "liberated" blankets and quilts. Wool-lined sleeping bags were often issued. Called a "mummy bag" owing to its form-fitting shape it was the equivalent of two blankets. Blankets and quilts could be wrapped around it within the water-resistant cover.

The troops' bedrolls, together with toilet items and (hopefully) dry clothing, were either kept in the squad truck or if unaccompanied by trucks they would be brought up at night from the company rear.

Field rations

Introduced in 1940, C-rations came in a cardboard carton with three meat units and three bread units each in a 12oz can. One M- and one B-unit

constituted a meal. The M-units were meat hash, meat stew with vegetables (carrots and potatoes), and meat stew with beans. In 1944 meat and spaghetti in tomato sauce, meat and noodles, pork and rice, frankfurters and beans, pork and beans, ham and lima beans, chicken and vegetables, and chopped ham, egg and potato were added and the unpopular hash dropped. The B-unit held five crackers, three sugar tablets, a beverage mix packet with instant coffee, powdered lemon drink (the acidic mix usually discarded), or bouillon soup powder. From 1944 cocoa powder and grape drink mix were added. Various hard candies were included, later replaced by disc candy or cookies. A paper accessory pack contained sugar, water-purification tablets, a flat wooden spoon, chewing gum, book matches, nine cigarettes, toilet paper, and a P-38 can opener. The C-rations were unpopular owing to their monotony, dense greasy contents, and inconvenient packaging. Eaten cold they were almost inedible. Soldiers learned fast that cans had to be opened *before* heating them over a fire or they would explode. Unopened cans could be boiled in a pot or helmet of water and heated nicely.

The K-ration was introduced in 1942, intended as an assault ration to be used for no more than 15 consecutive meals. However, it was not uncommon for troops to subsist on Ks for weeks and even months. Besides being monotonous they were deficient in vitamins, calories, and bulk, often leaving men hungry. The K-rations were issued in three pocket-size cartons designated breakfast, dinner, and supper although troops ate what was available or what they preferred.

"Breakfast" consisted of canned chopped ham and eggs or veal loaf, crackers, a dried fruit or cereal bar, water-purification tablets, four cigarettes, chewing gum, instant coffee, and sugar. "Dinner" was canned cheese spread, ham or ham and cheese, crackers, malted milk tablets or caramels, sugar, salt, cigarettes, book matches, chewing gum, and a powdered beverage packet (lemon, orange, or grape). "Supper" contained canned chicken paté, sausage, pork luncheon meat with carrot and apple or beef and pork, crackers, chocolate bar, toilet paper, cigarettes, chewing gum, and bouillon soup cube or powder.

ABOVE LEFT
Foxholes provided a pretty miserable existence and could become untenable in heavy rains or in areas with high water tables. Note the pack board in the upper right.

ABOVE
Regardless of heavy motorized engineer equipment, engineer troops were never far from a shovel. Here, engineers attempt to dig a drainage ditch beside a mud road in a near-futile effort to prevent it becoming even muddier.

Troops take a coffee break using a liberated coffee pot to brew up the GI's favorite beverage. Other items of cookware can be seen, including a frying pan. The 10-in-1 rations required cookware.

A rear area chow line with hot food served directly from the kitchen was a rare treat. The food may have been monotonous, but it was more bearable if served hot.

OPPOSITE
The Army went to major efforts to provide turkey and the traditional side dishes to the troops for Thanksgiving and Christmas. Here, grateful men chow down on the hood of a jeep.

The D-ration bar was issued for emergencies. Soldiers each carried one of the thick 4oz enriched chocolate bars. The special mixture would not melt or soften below 120°F (49°C). The "Logan bar" was specified to "taste little better than boiled potato" to prevent soldiers from snacking on it. Coupled with complaints of its effects on intestinal tracts and referred to as "Hitler's secret weapon," it was often discarded.

The 10-in-1 small group ration was introduced in mid-1943 to provide ten men three meals for one day. It was packed in two five-man cartons, which in turn packed four cartons in a 50lb box. While some items were ready-to-eat, most components required preparation and heating as they were provided in bulk 1lb cans or 8oz packages. Units were provided small cooking kits and one-burner stoves or they made do with "liberated" cooking equipment. Accessory items were cigarettes, matches, a can opener, toilet paper, soap, paper towels, and water-purification tablets. There were ten snack packets, with crackers, candy, beverage powder, sugar, and gum for lunch. Menus varied and included cereal, bacon, powdered eggs, crackers, corned beef hash, lima beans, string beans, beef in broth, steak and kidneys, liver loaf, luncheon loaf, corned beef, margarine, cooking lard,

fruit preserves, honey, raisins, chocolate bars, sugar, salt, milk powder or canned evaporated milk, coffee, and drink mix.

Even in combat, engineers were fed by the field kitchen when possible, often for breakfast and supper, and sometimes lunch, which was usually sandwiches. These were B-rations – foods issued in No. 10 (one-gallon) cans. Breakfast might be canned bacon or Spam with powdered eggs and pancakes or oatmeal. Supper might be stew or hash with whatever meat and vegetables were available, some type of vegetable (beans, peas, corn, carrots), and field-baked bread. Troops grew ill at the thought of Spam, which the cooks tried to prepare in every imaginable manner. Coffee was served with every meal.

The food would be carried out to positions and worksites in insulated Mermite containers. These held three insert containers separating foods. Often while in positions men paired off and one went to the kitchen with two mess kits. He would eat at the kitchen and then bring back his partner's now-cold chow or he might bring both of theirs back.

The steel helmet proved to be a valuable item. Set on the ground it served as a seat, which was better than sitting in the mud. Removed from its liner it could be used to dig foxholes and latrines, bail water out of the former, as a foxhole night soil pot, water bucket, washbowl, tent stake hammer, and cook pot (not recommended as the heat weakened the steel).

EXPERIENCE IN BATTLE

It is impossible in a book this size to describe all of the types of combat actions an engineer unit experienced. Their capabilities and missions were extremely diverse. An engineer platoon might undertake greatly different missions in a single day, not knowing what would be in store next. Three example missions that take place in France and Germany in 1944 are described here.

River crossing (France, August)
The river was not much more than a stream, about 80ft wide, and 4–5ft deep, but fast-flowing with a rocky bottom at its narrowest point. The engineer platoon leader and platoon sergeant lay atop a grassy knoll with a rifle company commander. The plan was simple, but not easy. The Germans were well dug-in farther downstream, to the right. A patrol had discovered this unprotected gap, covered only by occasional German patrols venturing through on the far side. The company CO reported that his scouts could see tripwires in the brush on the far shore indicating antipersonnel mines. The battalion wanted to put two companies across the stream and position them to attack the German flank before dusk.

A light pontoon company was bringing up ten 12ft-long deck sections with two pontoons per section, along with two M2 assault boats. The equipment was delivered to a grove of trees 500yds from the crossing site and assembly of the sections was begun by two of the engineer platoon's squads. The platoon leader oversaw this phase, but it was the two squad leaders who got the work done quickly and quietly. Even though an infantry patrol had approached the stream banks, the engineer platoon sergeant had the third squad double-check the approach for mines. This was accomplished by a visual search. The experienced engineers could easily detect disturbed soil and other signs of mine laying.

An assault boat was carried forward and a team paddled across, fighting the strong current. They strung a rope across the stream as they went. Once ashore, the mine detector team edged forward, working their way up the gentle slope. The mine detector operator was forced to walk upright while sweeping with the detector. Once he detected a mine he pinpointed the spot to a following man who probed to precisely locate and mark the location. Another engineer gingerly dug the mine out, always on the lookout for booby traps. Tripwires crossed their 4ft-wide route and these had to be cut after ensuring that they were not tension-release wires that would detonate a mine if cut. The cleared lane was marked by white cloth engineer tape tied to shrubs. They had to clear only about 60ft before they were out of the minefield. They had found two mines and cut three tripwires. In the meantime the assault boat ferried a rifle squad across and with the lane open they moved out to set up a couple of outposts. Several engineers brought up their two .30-cal. machine guns and set them up to cover the crossing site.

Groups of engineers and infantrymen began carrying up the pairs of light pontoons and deck sections. Each section was set parallel with the stream and upstream from the crossing site with ropes secured to it. The pontoons and deck sections were slid into the water and on order the upstream end was released and allowed to swing into the current. This carried the pontoons into position. Anchors fastened to the pontoons were emplaced upstream to hold the section in place. Each section was swung into the current like a pendulum and anchored in place. Once they started it only took 15 minutes. The access and exit ramps were quickly emplaced and they were then in business, with a bridge of 2ft-wide duckboards and rope

Infantrymen rush across a short infantry pontoon bridge. This one has rope handrails on both sides. They were often erected with only one handrail. Rather than anchoring the pontoon floats to the too-deep or too-muddy river bottom, they are anchored to an aerial steel cable. The strong current causes the bridge to warp, giving it a curved effect.

A medical aidman crosses an infantry footbridge. The passage of many troops leaves a slippery layer of mud making the handrails essential. Note the three yellow bands around the top of each handrail post to make it more visible in the dark.

handrails on both sides. The rest of the rifle platoon then crossed to further secure the far side.

As dusk approached the two rifle companies moved up and the troops filed across, taking only three minutes per company to deploy. They then moved on to their attack positions. The engineers' job was not finished. The mine-cleared lane was widened and luminous markers fastened to poles to mark the lane and bridge ramps. Pontoon anchors were constantly coming loose and had to be reset.

A green flare arching into the sky signaled the attack and mortars not far away began coughing. Before long walking wounded began to trickle back and the engineers assisted them over the bridge. When litter casualties began to be carried back the engineers relieved the litter bearers and hauled

F ASSAULT CROSSING

Emplacing bridges was one of the main jobs of combat engineer battalions, carried out by a light pontoon bridge company. Here, a light infantry footbridge has been emplaced to span a narrow river. Each 12ft-long, 2ft-wide bridge section is supported by two pontoon floats and includes an integral handrail. A rifle company is rapidly crossing to assemble in a flanking position to attack a German strongpoint from an unexpected direction. The far riverbank and nearshore ground is littered with antipersonnel mines. Engineers, who have been carried across the river by M2 assault boats, have cleared and marked a 4ft-wide lane with white cloth "engineer tape." Besides the standard eight paddles, the assault boats had a small Evinrude outboard motor available. The 16ft 8in. boats could carry two engineers and a 12-man rifle squad.

the casualties over the bridge. In the middle of the night a lone infantryman brought in three Germans and asked if he could turn them over to the engineers, as he had to get back. They shared cigarettes with the frightened and exhausted prisoners. Mermite cans of cold oatmeal, flapjacks, and coffee were brought up in the morning and that too was shared with the prisoners. They spent the morning marking the boundary of the minefield to aid future clearance. At mid-morning, word was received to recover the bridge and carry it back to the assembly area where it would be picked up. The war had moved on.

Barricade breaching (Germany, September)

Tanks entering small towns were encountering elaborate roadblocks. These not only slowed and hampered their movements, but blocked side streets to prevent the Shermans from bypassing the main streets, which were often unblocked and covered by antitank guns, Panzerschrecks, and Panzerfausts. They also encountered mines and booby traps which hampered accompanying infantry, and then there were stay-behind machine-gunners and snipers. The roadblocks were often found around curves and blind corners with tanks coming upon them unexpectedly. Halted, they might be taken under antitank fire and the infantry driven off by machine guns and snipers. Mortar or infantry-gun fire might then be dropped on them. They were usually located well inside the town so that they could not be detected as the Americans approached the outskirts. They had to enter and push into the town to locate the barricades.

An elaborate log street barricade in a German town. In this case the drop-gate did not have to be shattered with demolitions; the engineers merely hoisted it up using a dump truck's winch and secured it in place with steel cable.

Roadblocks could be crude, being simply piled rubble; cars, buses and wagons shoved into a pile; or railroad rails and ties embedded in the ground. The most common roadblocks were constructed out of heavy logs. A narrow trench would be cut across a street at a depth of 4ft or deeper, and logs 12–16in. in diameter were then inserted vertically with 8–12ft showing above ground, and often bound together by cable. They were braced on the German side with horizontal logs and timbers, and these were braced by dug-in angled logs. The approaches might be mined and booby-trapped. The mines could be buried in unpaved streets, in holes cut in asphalt and camouflaged with a layer of light rubble, or simply laid exposed on the street.

Barricades could be blasted down by 75mm and 105mm tank gunfire, but this required a large number of rounds, expended valuable ammunition, and required the tanks to remain exposed for too long. When roadblocks became a problem owing to their strength and numbers, the engineers were called.

Engineer squads were organized into three or four demolition teams. While there was only one designated demolition man, most (if not all) had been trained for the role. Time was of the essence and there was no finesse or precise quantities of explosives calculated.

A demo team might accompany a platoon of four or five tanks, itself supported by an infantry platoon. Depending on the number of avenues of approach, two or three demo teams might be employed. They would alternate blasting roadblocks and preparing charges.

The demo team would link up with their assigned platoon in the tank company's assembly area the night before the attack. They coordinated where their position would be in the formation, methods of marking targets, how the demolitions would be transported, and means of communicating with the tank platoon leader.

Just before dawn, after hot coffee and cold K-rations, the assault group moved into its attack position. Artillery opened up at first light and tank and infantry machine guns began working over the town's outskirts. Mortar smoke began impacting on the edge of the village. After giving the billowing smoke time to develop into an effective screen the tanks moved out with two or three on either side of the road, machine guns blazing. German mortar rounds soon began to land behind the assault group. Bursts of red and white tracers streaked out of the town, forcing the infantrymen to bunch up behind the tanks, but remaining in their 16.5in.-wide tread tracks to avoid antipersonnel mines. More mortar rounds impacted and a couple of infantrymen went down.

Reaching the edge of the town they now became concerned with short-range fire. A Panzerfaust, burst of machine-gun fire, or grenades

Besides floats, treadway bridge sections with multiple pontoons could be launched from the bridge's end using an A-frame with block and tackle.

could come from anywhere. The infantry would move ahead ensuring there were no Panzerfaust-armed enemy lying in wait, whilst the tanks covered them. If the infantry were taken under fire they fell back and the tanks opened up. They accomplished as much with their machine guns as they did with their main guns.

Ahead, around the shallow curve of a street, a log roadblock could be seen. Wrecked vehicles and rubble blocked side streets, preventing tanks from turning into them for cover. There was little doubt that an ambush awaited. The tanks sent streams of tracers through windows and doors and then infantrymen cautiously advanced. A machine gun from a second-floor window cut down two. A flurry of rifle fire opened up and rifle grenades were launched. A tank moved down the street to fire into the window.

With the houses cleared the engineers rushed forward assisted by a couple of riflemen. They were on the lookout for signs of mines and booby traps. They set two 53lb crates containing 48 1lb TNT charges on the ground directly against the vertical logs 4ft apart. It was overkill, but there was no doubt they would do the job. It was not known what reinforced the barricade's other side. They had drilled a hole in the center of each crate's lid with a detcord drill. A 7ft length of detcord was prepared with a blasting cap on each end. To the middle of this was taped two "standard firing systems:" 9in. of timed fuse with a cap on one end and a friction igniter on the other, giving a 30-second delay. The two caps were taped to the 7ft-long detcord. With the crates in place the ends of the detcord were inserted in the lid holes and into one of the TNT blocks' fuse well. Both fuse igniters were pulled and the demo men ran for it as the infantry opened up with suppressive fire at windows and other positions. Snipers fired at them as they rushed in a crouch back down the street, throwing themselves behind a rubble pile.

The deafening detonation literally blew the barricade to splinters and exploded nearby booby traps and mines through sympathetic detonation. The engineers dashed back to the breach accompanied by infantrymen to check the other side for mines. There was only a modest crater as the explosives had not been tamped (topped with sandbags to direct the blast inward). The infantrymen rushed through and began clearing the street as the lead tank rolled through the gap. It had taken just five minutes from when the engineers rushed forward to emplace the charges. The demo team had begun checking houses for booby traps when a messenger arrived telling them there was another barricade ahead.

G **STREET ANTITANK BARRICADE BREACHING**

Two combat engineers, covered by an infantryman who has helped them emplace two crates containing 48 1lb TNT changes, prepare to detonate the charges in order to breach a typical vertical log street barricade. Such barricades were built in large numbers and often reinforced on the other side by angled logs. They could be booby-trapped or mined on either side. An ambush or snipers might also be waiting on the other side. Emplacing such demolition charges was not as dangerous as it may seem in that bullet hits would not detonate TNT or plastic explosives. The two crates are linked by detcord and will be ignited by double "standard firing systems" with timed fuse and friction igniters to ensure detonation. The detonation of almost 100lb of TNT will shatter the barricade, but caused little cratering, especially since the charges were not tamped with sandbags. An M4 Sherman tank could easily pass through by bursting through the barricade's remnants, whether the street was cratered or not.

The sign in the photograph reads:

THE LONGEST TACTICAL BRIDGE BUILT
THE FIRST ACROSS THE RHINE
CONSTRUCTED BY
291 ENGR C BN
988 TDWY CO
998 TDWY CO

At the time the first and longest (1,100ft) tactical bridge to be built across the Rhine was built in partnership by the 291st Engineer Combat Battalion and the 988th and 998th Engineer Treadway Bridge Companies. Bridges on main routes that were left in place for a time often had "bragging rights" signs erected.

Roadblock clearance (Germany, November)

The platoon sergeant watched the litter bearers carry off the platoon leader, who was suffering from severe trench foot. He hadn't taken care of himself, being more concerned for his men. The sergeant hated seeing him go. The lieutenant had the ability to keep the men motivated and got a lot out of them when they were almost spent. The sergeant tried to be tough on the men, but he had entered the Army with most them and held his the rank because he had been foreman of a house-framing crew. The 44-man platoon was down to 32 men. At least they were better off than the rifle platoons, he reminded himself.

They had been fighting through the Hürtgen Forest for weeks now, losing up to three men on some days, mostly to injuries caused by the cold and wet weather, but mines, booby traps, snipers, and tree-bursting artillery and mortars had contributed. They were ceaselessly cold and wet. The mess section was not doing much of a job he thought. Seven men and all they managed to get up to his platoon were "mystery stews" – unidentifiable concoctions made by combining C-rations and 10-in-1 rations. It was invariably cold and congealed. They had a little German gasoline stove and some liberated pots and they would try to heat the stuff up. Sometimes it was after dark when the chow arrived, when they were not permitted fires. Cold coffee was the worst.

Every night they dug 3ft-deep rectangular two-man holes, unless they took over holes abandoned by the advancing infantry or retreating Germans. German holes were commonly lice-infested, but at least they sometimes found abandoned cans of really good chocolate, liverwurst, and hard sausage. Over their own holes they laid three or four logs crossways, covered these with lengthwise logs, and spread shelter-halves.

The Germans were fighting a costly delaying action and letting the weather take its toll. The degree of imagination they encountered in minefields and booby traps was disturbing. They never knew what to expect.

Pushes had typically begun at dawn, but now it was mid-morning before things got moving. Everything was slowed down by the weather and fatigue. Everything was late and slow to coordinate, and it was 1000hrs before the infantry's advance began. There were signs that the Germans were pulling out, but there would no doubt be rearguards, mines, booby traps, and obstacles to overcome (see Osprey Warrior 146: *German Pionier 1939–45* for the German perspective of establishing these obstacles).

The engineer platoon would support the lead rifle company. The other two companies would be echeloned to the right and left. The point company would be navigating along a secondary road, which would be dangerous because the Germans would no doubt have left surprises along the dirt road. This was necessary though because the rugged terrain and dense vegetation was so difficult to remain oriented in. If the point company met stout resistance, the flanking companies echeloned to the rear could attack the enemy from a flank. The remaining flank company could maneuver to meet a German counterattack from another direction or otherwise support the main attack. Three Sherman tanks followed the point company.

An engineer unit's convoy forms up in two columns. Only one lane is open to traffic heading from the front.

The German defenders had mostly fallen back, but (as usual) snipers were abundant. Two engineer squads followed the company while a squad remained in the rear with the cargo truck and the one remaining dump truck preparing demo changes, ready to bring more forward. Normally the battalion's own pioneer platoon would perform this duty. However, that platoon was down to 11 men and was being used solely to haul ammo forward.

A messenger came back reporting that a stream was ahead; almost certainly the crossing would be mined. The mine detector would be worthless as it was not waterproof. They would have to probe for them the old-fashioned way. Two engineers pulled on wader boots and ventured forward probing with long poles. Two Tellermines ("T-mines") were discovered in the stream with long crossed sticks wired to the bottom to prevent them from settling in the mud. About 30yds up the

Mine, booby trap, and dud clearance were very common engineer tasks. Here a *Tellermine* has been uncovered and defused. The engineer is checking beneath it for antilifting devices. His comrades obviously trust him.

road an obviously poorly camouflaged mine was found. There was little doubt it was booby-trapped. A ½lb TNT block fitted with a standard firing system was simply set atop the T-mine and detonated after the squad leader shouted "Fire in the hole!" three times. The explosion was more powerful than a German 150mm artillery round.

The poorly camouflaged mine alerted the engineers that there might be well-camouflaged mines ahead. The rifle company continued, being cautioned to be on the lookout for antipersonnel mines and booby traps. The engineers had to clear not only the road itself, but either side of it as well. The mine detector was working well enough. Probing had not discovered any wooden or glass mines. The uncovered T-mines were blown in place. Up ahead there was an explosion. Three litters were soon carried past with the victims of an S-mine, a "bouncing bitch." One engineer squad moved up and cleared the area where the S-mine had taken its toll. As they approached the area a booby-trapped grenade detonated, claiming another casualty. More S-mines and booby traps were found. At one point boards, tree limbs, and fence posts had been piled and booby-trapped with grenades, one obvious and two hidden. This crude roadblock halted tanks simply because they would not plow through it for fear of mines. It was not uncommon for such simple roadblocks to result in a barrage of Panzerfausts once the tank halted. The area was cleared without further casualties.

Scouts immediately reported a more significant roadblock ahead, an abatis of dozens of felled trees criss-crossed down the road's length. There was little doubt it was mined and booby-trapped. The mine detector proved worthless, as the Germans had thrown scrap metal and cans into the fallen firs, making it impossible to detect mines. The engineers gingerly picked their way through, disarming booby traps and placing crates of TNT, which they linked with detcord. The troops were pulled back and eight crates of TNT were simultaneously detonated. Tree limbs and wooden chunks rained down for half a minute.

The lead Sherman immediately charged on through and several Panzerfausts blasted out of the trees. The tank burst into flames and most of the crew bailed out. The engineer platoon sergeant was among those who helped drag off the wounded crew, and he was struck down by machine-gun fire. German resistance was short-lived, as artillery began to barrage the enemy position within minutes.

THE AFTERMATH OF BATTLE

The engineer's own medic and an infantry medic frantically worked on the wounded. The platoon sergeant had caught two slugs in the right leg. They slit open his trousers and long johns. The gaping exit and the small entry wounds were dusted with sulfanilamide or "sulfa" power, a small packet

of which was carried in his first-aid pouch. The medics had more. He was also given eight Sulfadiazine "wound tablets." They had to be taken with a lot of water, which was critical. If water was not available soldiers were taught to wait until it was before taking the tablets and told to use wine if available. His own field dressing was applied to the exit wound and gauze pads applied to the entry wounds.

A cartoon from an engineer unit newspaper depicts the near-comic reaction and confusion the staff endured during a nighttime artillery barrage.

To help prevent shock the wounded were bundled in blankets, their feet elevated, and bootlaces cut in order not to restrict circulation. The wounds were becoming painful and an aidman injected a morphine syrette into the sergeant's thigh. The one-dose syrette was in a little toothpaste-like tube with a long needle. An opium derivative and highly addictive, morphine addiction proved to be a challenge for many recovering veterans. To prevent overdosing, the used syrette was pinned to the patient's collar by bending the needle. Sometimes "M" was marked on the forehead.

The wounded tanker had taken fragments in the legs and belly. The belly wound prevented him from receiving morphine and wound tablets, as a throat wound would have. Blood loss was severe, and an aidman inserted a needle in the forearm and hung a 1pt plasma bottle on a bush's limb to keep it suspended. It might too be hung on a pole or rifle jammed into the ground by its bayonet or simply held by an aidman or an able casualty. Plasma could be kept without refrigeration while blood spoiled within three days even when refrigerated. The Army also developed dried plasma, which kept longer and was reconstituted with distilled water. Plasma was responsible for keeping thousands alive.

The wounded were carried by litter bearers or jeep ambulances to the battalion aid station, and then on to the regimental aid station. From

Two medical aidmen were attached to each engineer company from the battalion medical detachment. Other platoon personnel would assist when a man was seriously wounded.

there they were sent to the medical battalion's clearing company supporting the regiment. There were increased care capabilities at each echelon rearward. From there they would be transported to an evacuation hospital.

Decorations were few, and very few for valor were awarded to engineers, especially the top two, the Medal of Honor and the Distinguished Service Cross. The Silver Star and Bronze Star Medals were more common, and the latter could also be awarded for meritorious service in a combat zone, not just for valor. The Purple Heart was bestowed on personnel wounded or killed in action. All personnel serving in Europe, North Africa, and the Middle East between December 1941 and March 1946 were presented the European-African-Middle Eastern Campaign Medal or "EAME Medal." A small bronze star device was authorized for each designated campaign the soldier participated in. The World War II Victory Medal or "Victory Ribbon" was authorized for all personnel who served between December 1941 and December 1946. After the war troops serving in Europe were awarded the Army of Occupation Medal from May 9, 1945 to 1955 in Germany and Austria, 1947 in Italy, and in Berlin until 1990. The Good Conduct Medal required three years of exemplary behavior, efficiency, and fidelity on active duty, or one year in wartime.

The wounded would be carried to the battalion aid station, but first had to be stabilized to the degree possible in that era. Here, plasma is given to a wounded man. One of the platoon's dump trucks might be used to carry the wounded to the rear.

BIBLIOGRAPHY

Beck, Alfred M., Bortz, Abe, Lynch, Charles W., and Weld, Ralph F., *United States Army in World War II, The Corps of Engineers: The War Against Germany* (Center of Military History: Washington, DC, 1985)

Gawne, Jonathan, *Spearheading D-Day: American Special Units of the Normandy Invasion* (Histoire & Collections: Paris, 1998)

Giles, Janice H., *The Damned Engineers* (Houghton Miffin: Boston, 1970)

Pergrin, Colonel David E., and Hammel, Eric, *First Across the Rhine: The Story of the 291st Engineer Combat Battalion in France, Belgium, and Germany* (Atheneum: New York, 1989)

Radford, Albert E., and Redford, Laurie S., *Unbroken Line: The 51st Engineer Combat Battalion – From Normandy to Munich* (Cross Mountain Publishing: Woodside, CA, 2002)

Scott, John L., *Combat Engineer* (American Liberty Press: Baltimore, 1999)

Southergill, Norman, *A Combat Engineer Remembers* (Trafford Publishing: Bloomington, IN, 2006)

Stanton, Shelby, *US Army Uniforms of World War II* (Stackpole Books: Harrisburg, PA, 1991)

Windrow, Richard, and Hawkins, Tim, *The World War II GI: US Army Uniforms 1941–45* (Motorbooks International: Osceola, WI, 1993)

Wong, John B., *Battle Bridges: Combat River Crossings in World War II* (Trafford Publishing: Victoria, Canada, 2006)

US Army, *Engineer Troops*, FM 5-5 (October 11, 1943)

INDEX

Figures in **bold** refer to illustrations